# ITALY

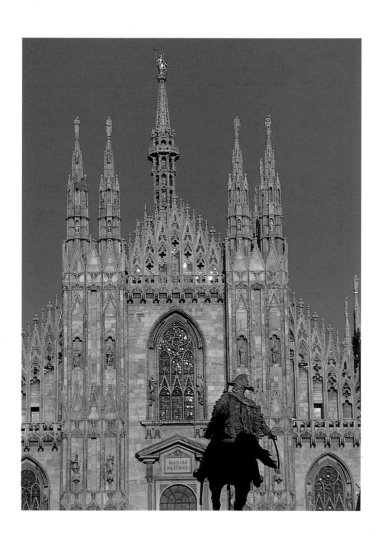

SMITHMARK

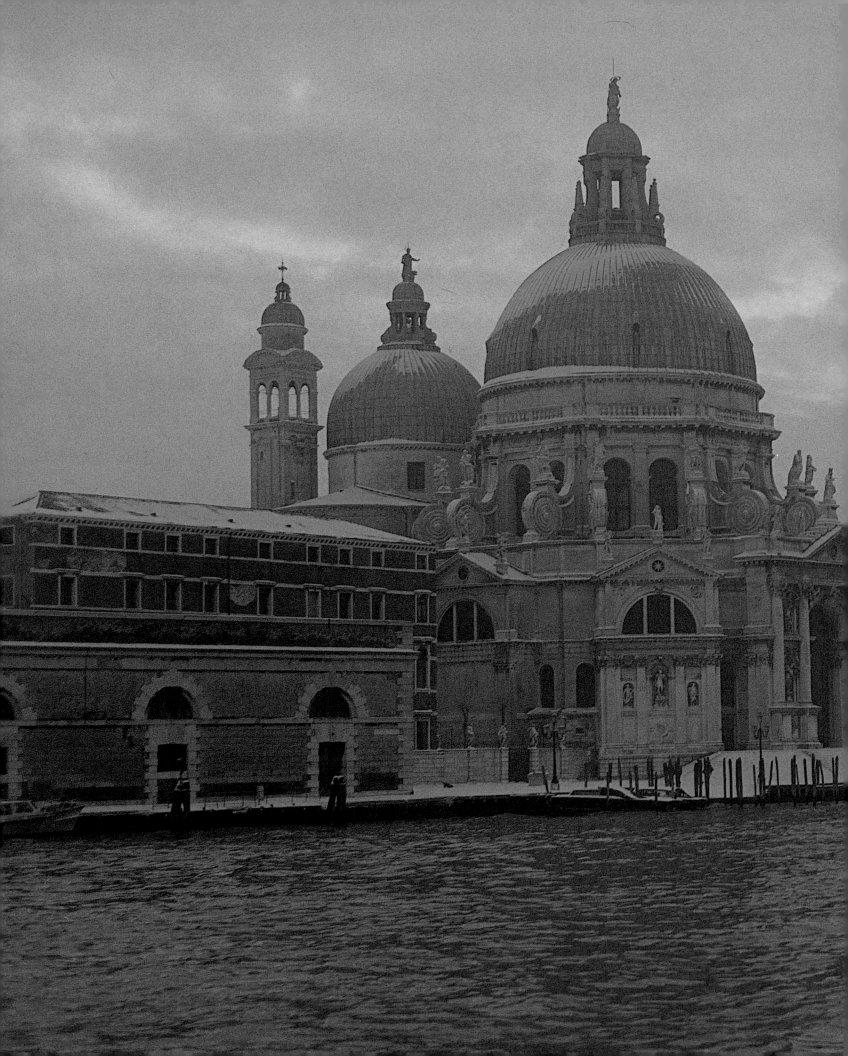

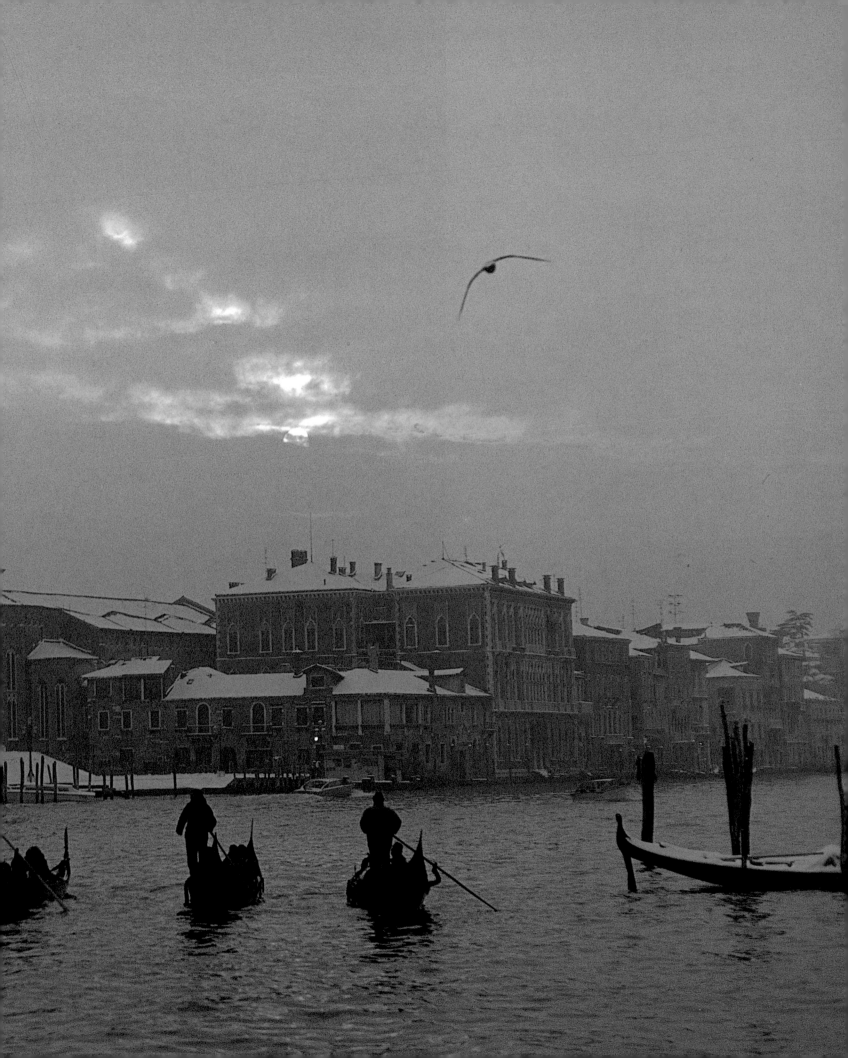

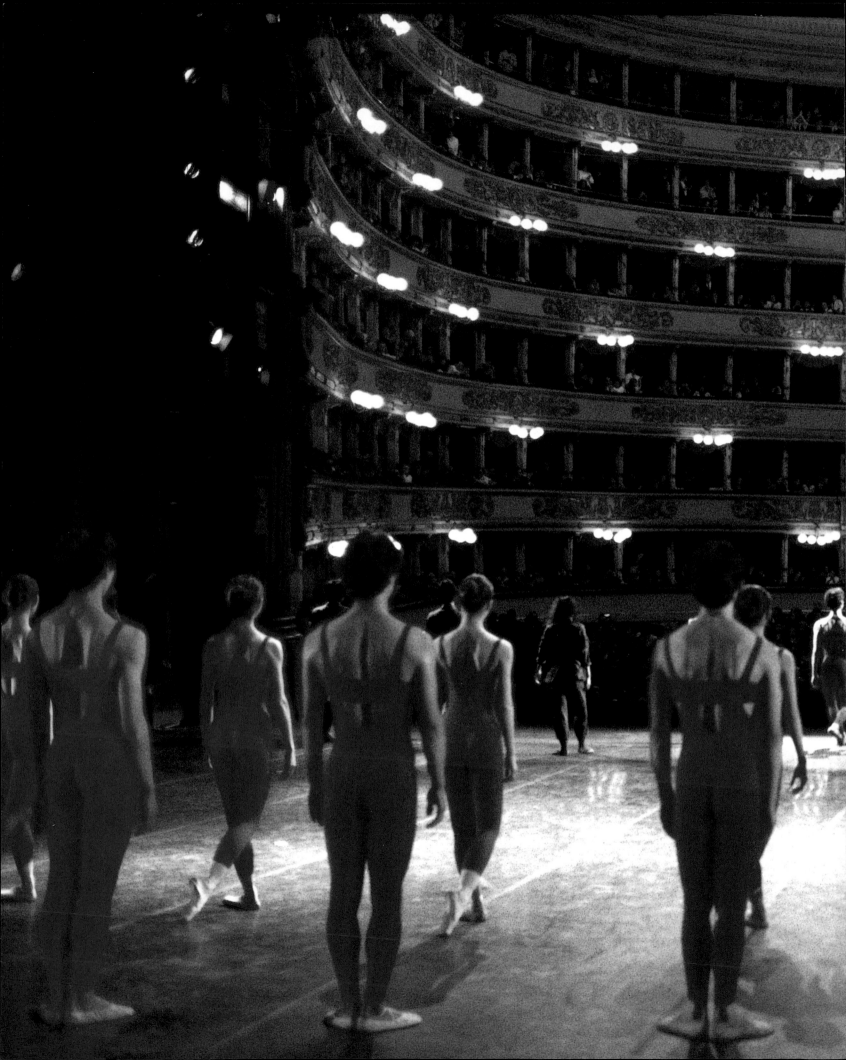

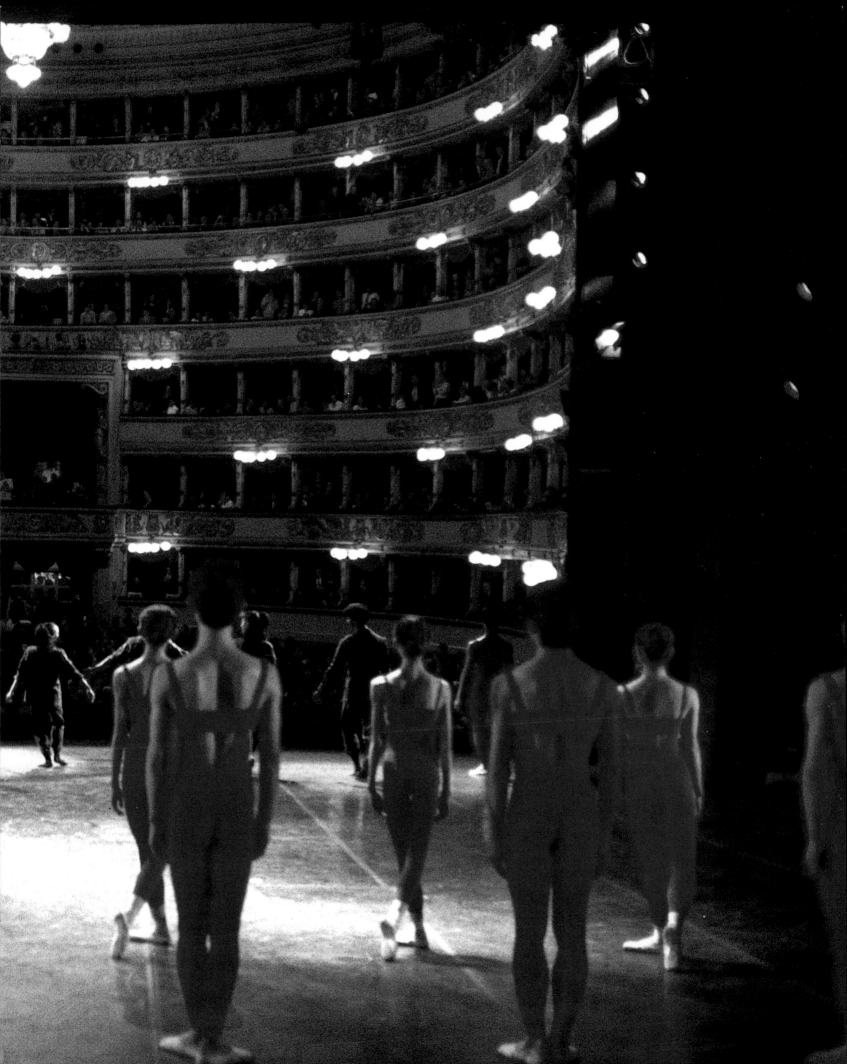

*Text*
Fabio Bourbon
Paola Aghini

*Translation*
Richard Reville

*Graphic design*
Patrizia Balocco

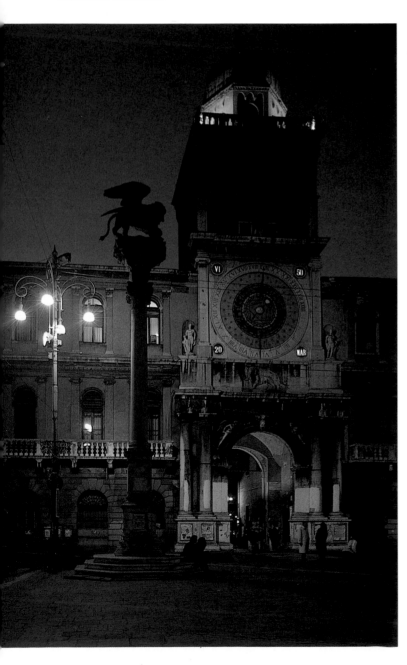

# Contents

Pride in the Past and the Future ...............*page 32*
An Iridescent Fable ......................................*page 82*
The Mountains: Enormous Sentries..........*page 108*

2-3 *A masterpiece of Venetian Baroque architecture, the Church of Santa Maria della Salute is one of the largest buildings on the Grand Canal.*

4-5 *La Scala is the pride of Milan and perhaps the most famous opera house in the world.*

6 *In the heart of Padua, Piazza dei Signori and its magnificent monuments symbolize the city's former power.*

7 *The gardens of Palazzo Reale, decorated with flower beds and neo-classic statues, provide a green oasis in the heart of Turin.*

8-9 *A point above the Greek theater of Taormina affords a splendid view of the Sicilian coast, dominated by Mt. Etna.*

10-11 *The beach at Budelli in Sardinia is known for the warm pink color of its coralline sand.*

12-13 *Sunrise highlights the majesty of Cima Tosa, part of the Brenta Group within the Dolomite Range.*

14-15 *The medieval towers of San Gimignano loom over the city, bathed in the warm light of the setting sun.*

This edition published in 1993 by SMITHMARK Publishers Inc., 16 East 32nd Street, New York, NY 10016.

SMITHMARK books are available for bulk purchase for sales promotion and premium use. For details write or call the Manager of Special Sales, SMITHMARK Publishers InC., 16 East 32nd Street, New York, NY 10016; (212) 532-6600.

First published by Edizioni White Star. Title of the original edition: Italia, genio antico e moderna Intraprendenza. © World copyright 1992 by Edizioni White Star. Via Candido Sassone 22/24, 13100 Vercelli, Italy.

ISBN 0-8317-4830-3

Printed in Singapore by Singapore National Printers. Color separations by Magenta, Lit. Con., Singapore.

Bourbon, Fabio.
   Italy / Fabio Bourbon.
     p.  cm.
   ISBN 0-8317-4830-3
   1. Italy--Description and travel--1975- 2. Italy--Civilization.
  3. Cities and towns--Italy--Guidebooks.  I. Title.

DG430.2.B69  1993
914.604'927--dc20
                         92-35282
                             CIP

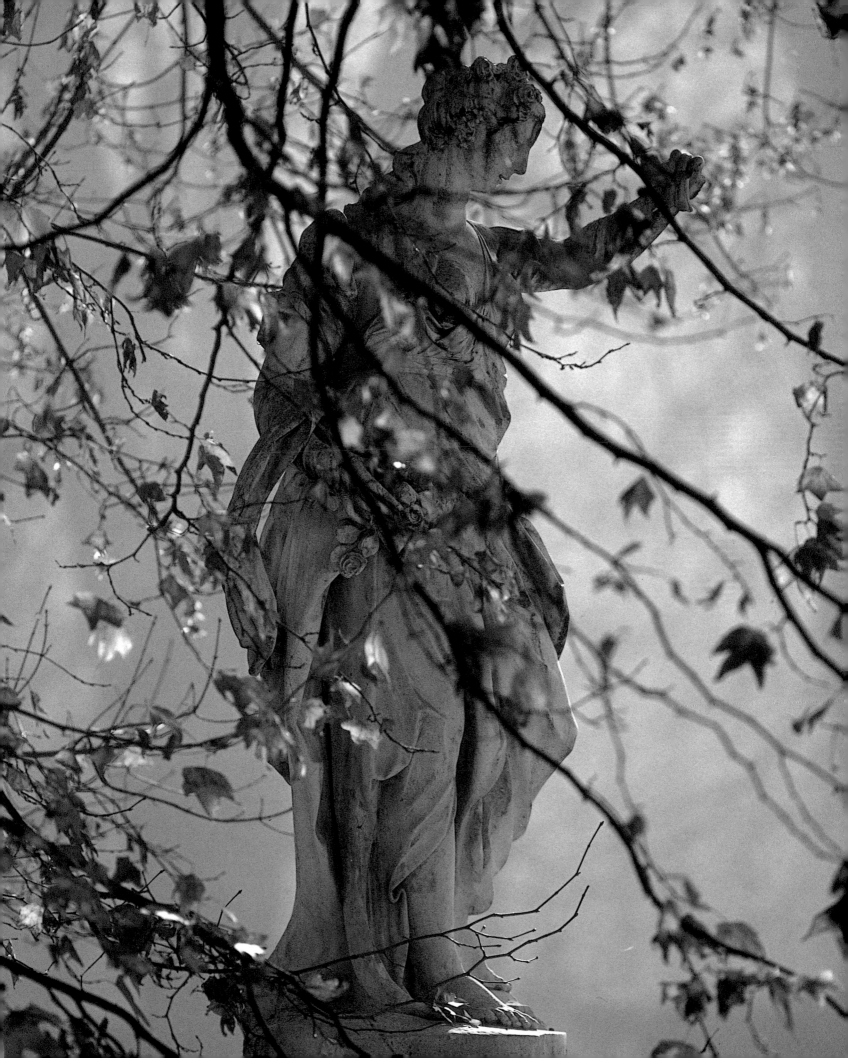

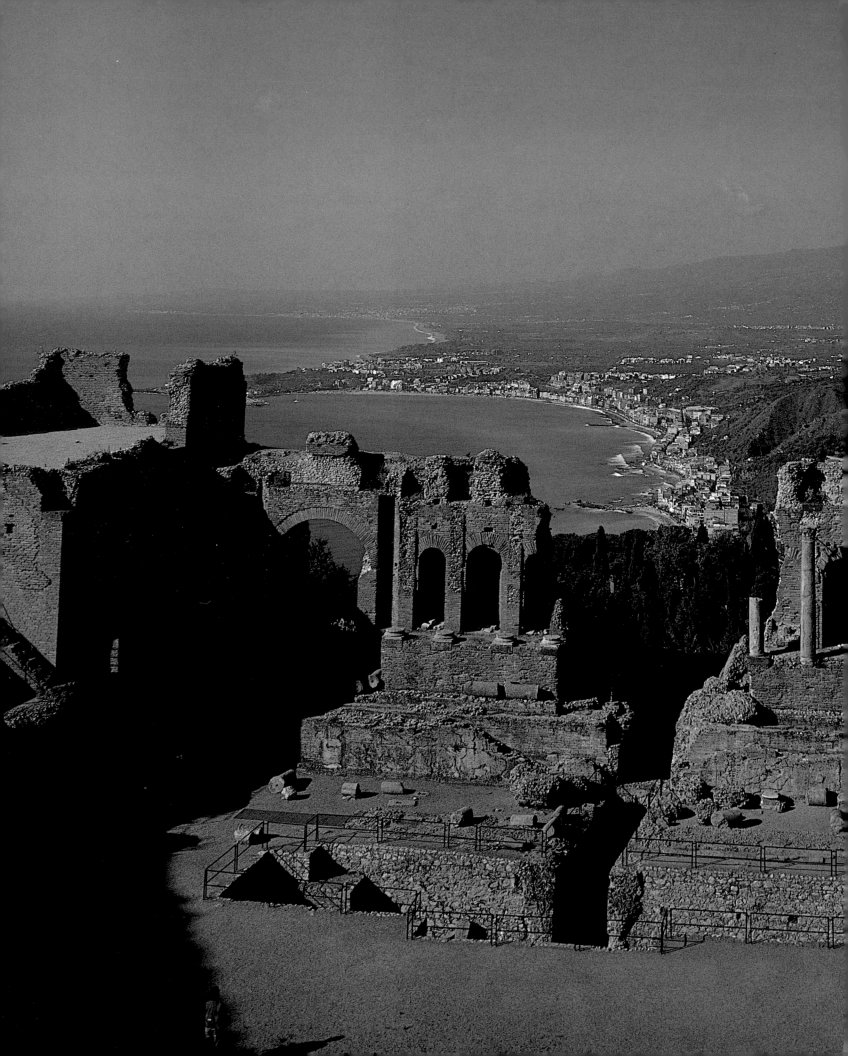

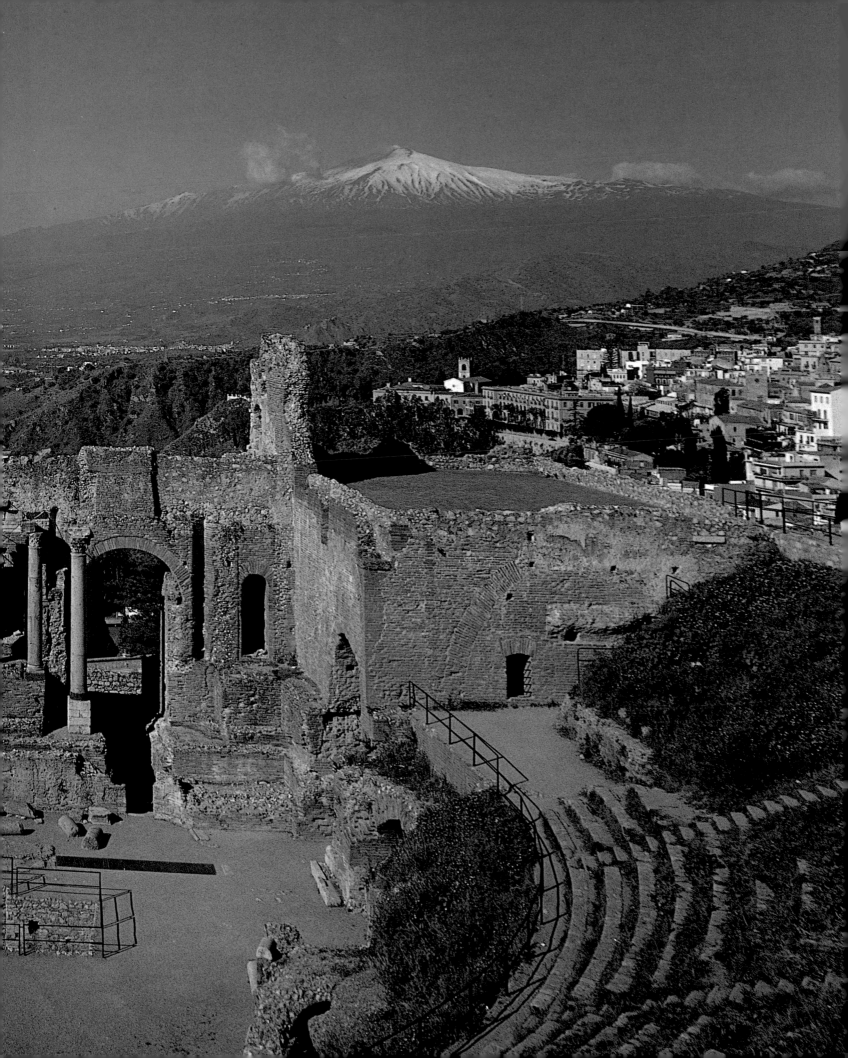

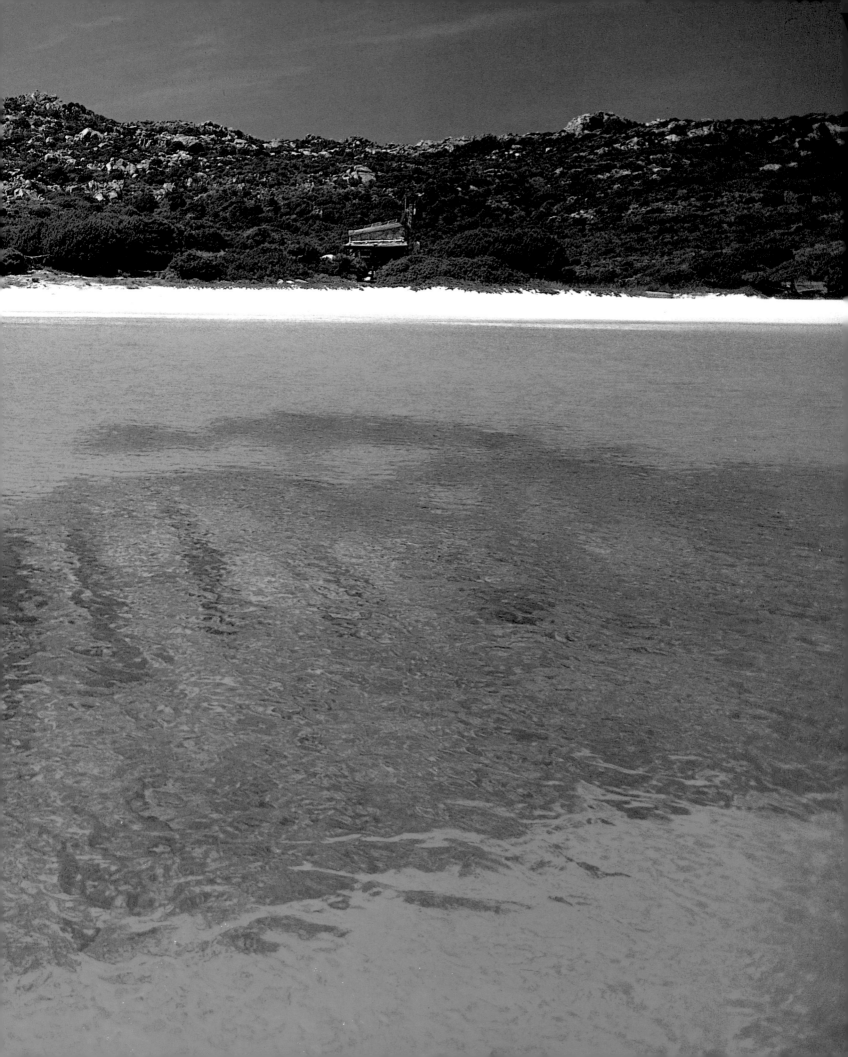

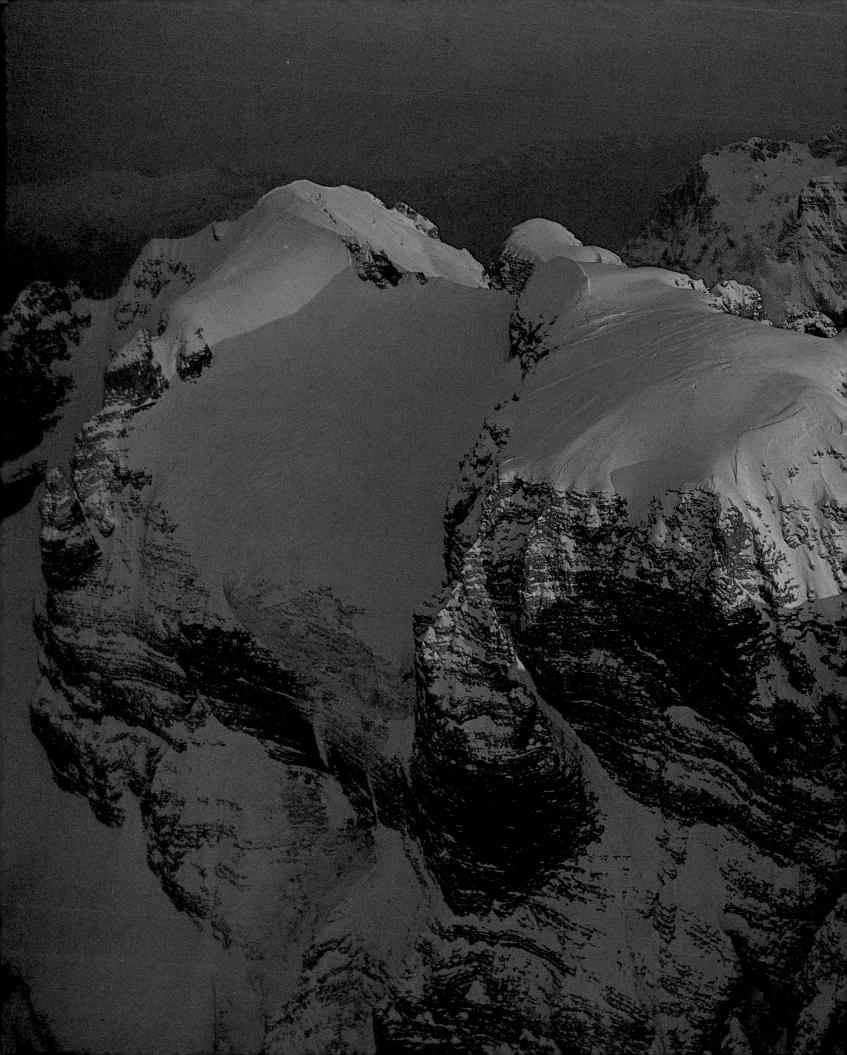

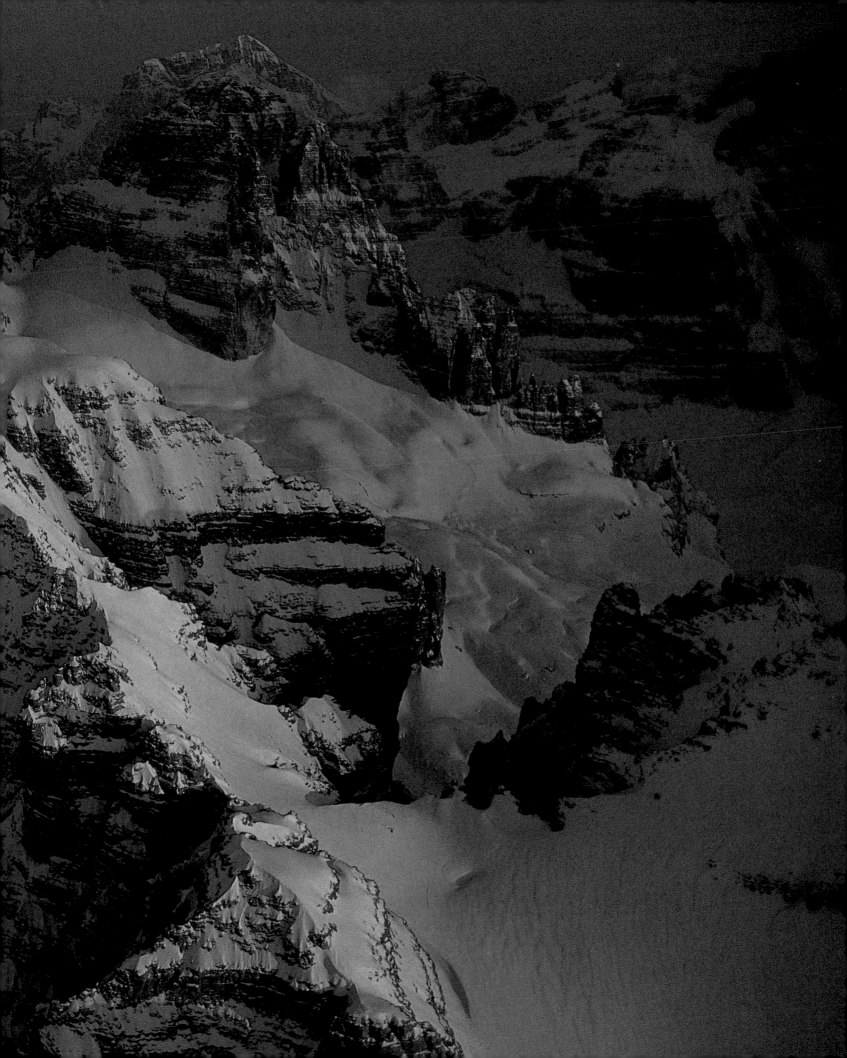

# Introduction

In 1965, while orbiting the Earth high above Italy, the crew of Gemini 7 could clearly see that the country was shaped much like a boot. Defined by its position and peculiar shape, the Italian peninsula stands out as the most unusual geographical formation in Europe. Joined by Alpine mountains to the central regions of the old continent, the country reaches down to the very heart of the Mediterranean Sea, almost forming a bridge between Europe and Africa. By strange coincidence, and due to its pronounced elongation along a northwest-southeast axis, its extremities are equidistant in terms of both longitude and latitude.

Because of its location and physical features, Italy was the "caput mundi" of Roman civilization, a land much sought after by neighboring war-mongering populations. Later it was the cradle of the Renaissance of the Western world. It was the object of a revived nationalistic spirit during the mid-19th century. After being freed from two decades of dictatorship, it became the protagonist of an exceptional post-war economic boom. Italy now carries the image of an industrious nation in the avant-garde in the fields of technology and tourism.

The peninsula offers a variety of scenery, ranging from splendid mountains to barren, sun-drenched expanses where the only sound is the chirping of cicadas. Over and above its natural marvels, this land also offers the fascination of ancient civilizations and cultural movements that have animated it and made Italians so extraordinarily lively and varied. It is precisely this heterogeneity that makes Italy so fascinating to the foreigner.

People have always identified Italy with pizza, macaroni, and the mandolin. But cross the frontier, and it is easy to forget the things usually identified with Italy. To deny these preconceived ideas, begin your itinerary at Trieste, which Umberto Saba describes as having ". . .a sullen grace. When it pleases, it is like a course, greedy youngster with blue eyes

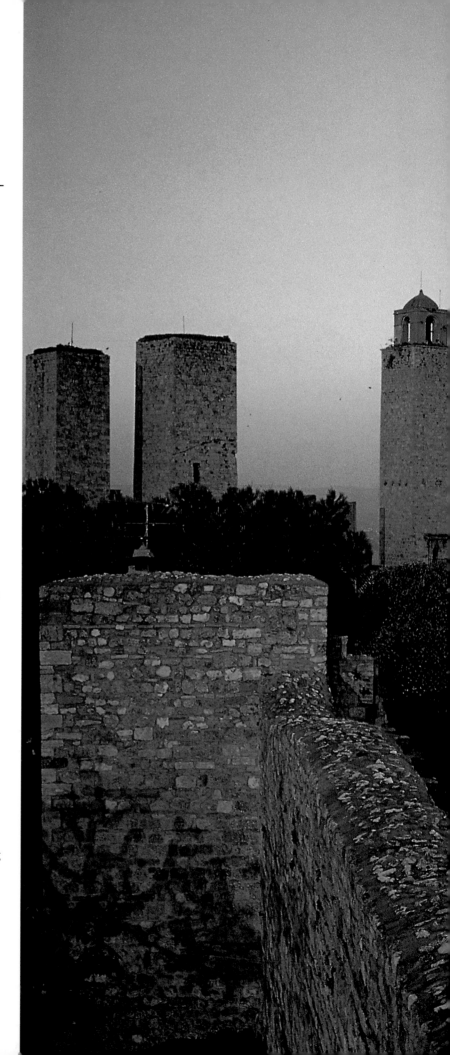

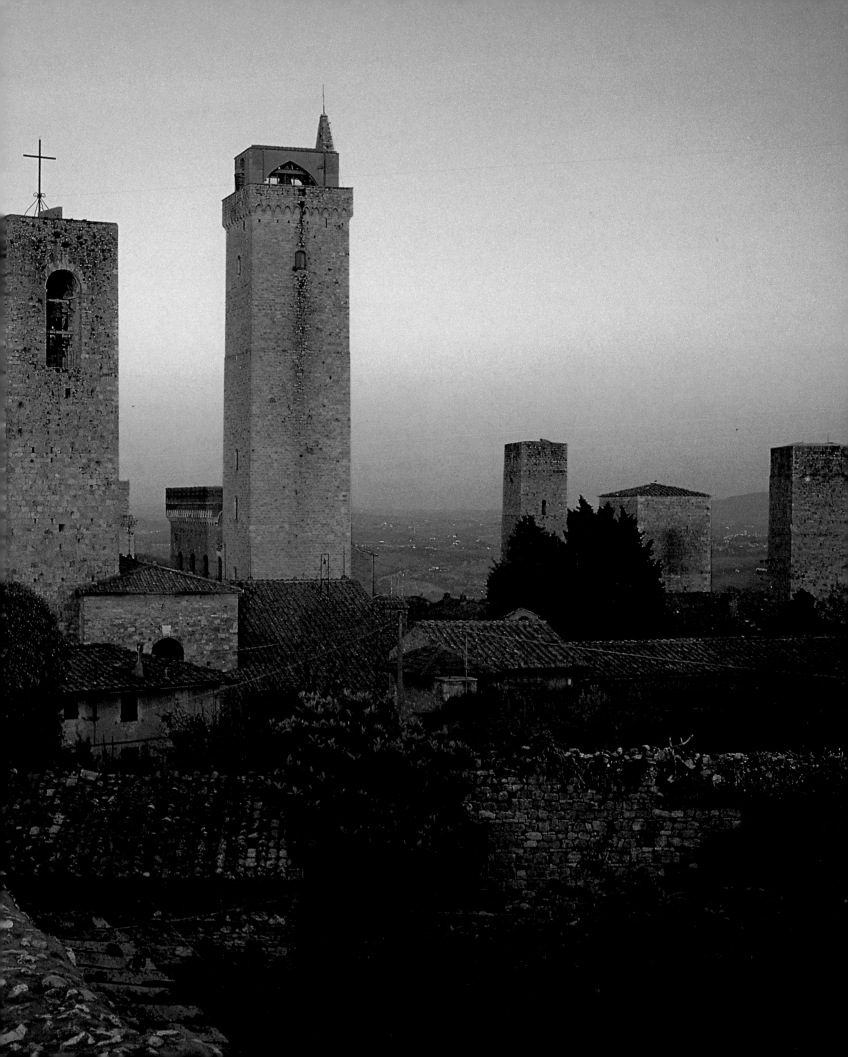

and hands that are too big to present a lady with a flower; like a love affair tainted by jealousy. . . ." This is the way the traveler sees it. The first impression is of a rugged landscape typical of the Carso: grey rocks eroded by rain and hollowed out here and there by shallow "dolinas" perched along a stretch of sea from which the Vittoria lighthouse emerges. This slender construction was built on the headland where an Austrian fort once blocked the road to Italy.

Here, the sea is both open and enclosed, merging on the horizon with the tip of Istrian Peninsula and that of Friuli, where the Isonzo River flows to the Gulf. The symbol of the city, San Giusto's Cathedral, is not harmonious to the view because of the union of two parallel buildings dedicated to Our Lady of the Assumption and to the patron saint. The center of town life is Piazza Unita d'Italià, which opened at the end of the 19th century directly onto the sea. This monumental setting is surrounded on three sides by some of the most famous public and private buildings of the second half of the 19th century, such as the town hall and the headquarters of the Lloyd Triestino Insurance Company. If one follows the merry comings and goings of the crowd that invades the square during the fine season and walks along the sea front enlivened by all types of quays and buildings, one arrives at the Peschiera Pier with its enormous fish market. By boarding a boat from the busy port, one can reach Venice, a destination that has enchanted travelers of all times and all generations.

Arriving by sea, one enjoys the best view of this city, which seems to give itself generously but whose soul, in fact, is somewhat hidden. The emotion felt when landing in the "Serenissima," admiring its monuments or walking through the tight maze of tiny streets and "calli," is an immutable sensation even for those who know this town very well because the city always looks different, as if it were reborn each day with new verve and color. From the pier where the ships arrive, one passes between two Byzantine columns surmounted by the statue of San Theodoro and the lion of St. Mark, symbol of this ancient maritime republic. Beyond the Doge's Palace with its delicate stone lacework decoration is the shade of the majestic bell tower. From here one can see the Basilica, a magnificent Oriental dream which was built and decorated with the innumerable works of art brought from the East by sailing ships. The interior with its golden mosaics and soft light takes on added charm if seen while attending one of the classical music concerts periodically held there. Only then, without the hubbub of the tourists and filled only with intangible musical notes, does one understand the true spirituality of the church.

16 *With its Baroque garden containing a number of fountains and elegant statues, Palazzo Pfanner is doubtless one of the most charming patrician mansions in Lucca.*

17 *Palazzo Giusti in Verona has a splendid 18th-century Italian garden designed with mazes and long boulevards of cypresses in accordance with the taste and style of its time.*

18-19 *Count Carlo III Borromeo built the palace and terraced gardens of Isola Bella for his wife Isabella in the 16th century. Today they are the main tourist attraction on Lake Maggiore.*

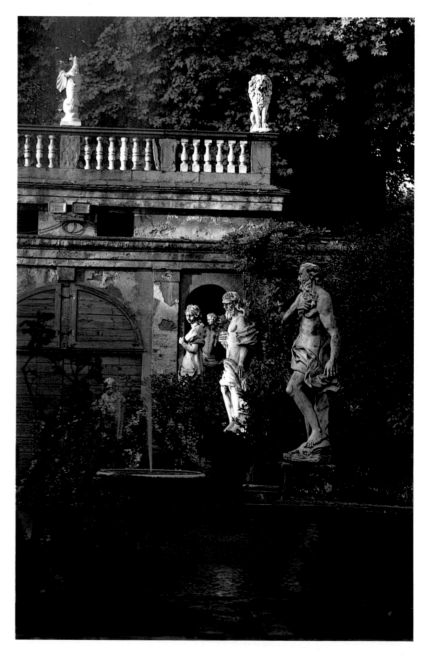

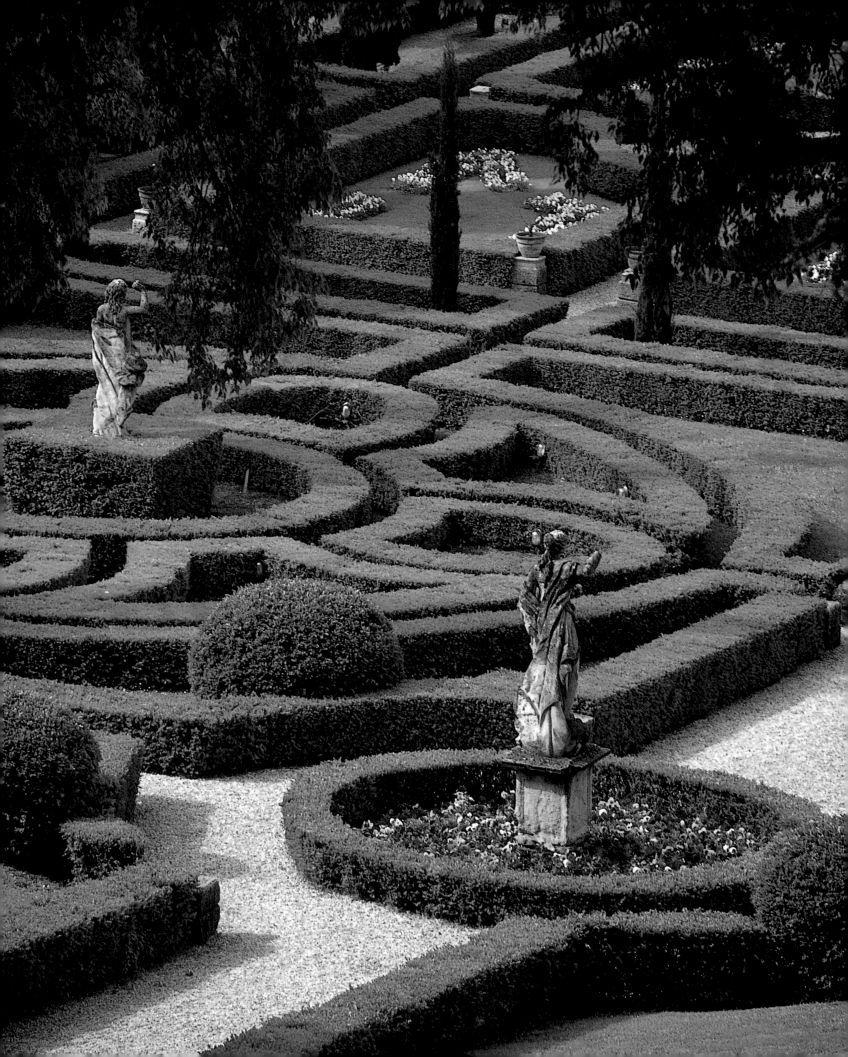

Venice does not end in St. Mark's Square. On foot or by gondola, and never with haste, one only has to proceed into any of its "calli" to come across historic buildings full of art treasures or a bar that has hosted famous names of the past. If, however, a traveler tires of monuments and churches and wants an alternative, he or she can also find pleasure in visiting Venice's most secret corners or relax in the sun in a little square before continuing the tour to Punta della Dogana, where a visit to the church of the Madonna della Salute is a must. Here, in the shady sacristy, the eyes of the guests in Tiepolo's well-known painting of the Marriage Feast of Cana seem to follow those of the observer. An evocative atmosphere can be felt everywhere, and this explains how the Regata Storica and the fancy-dress Carnival can become unique spectacles. The latter is perhaps the only event in which Venetians mix willingly with tourists.

Although it is not far away, Padua offers quite a contrast to Venice. Of all the cities in the Veneto region, it has perhaps the least monumental appearance, although it abounds with valuable works of art. The Cappella degli Scrovegni has a famous cycle of paintings by Giotto, quite distinct from the works the artist did in Assisi because of their deeper lyricism and a more careful description of the psychology of his subjects. Not far from here are the vegetable and flower stalls of Piazza delle Erbe. Overlooking this square, Palazzo della Ragione contains a colossal wooden statue of a horse, an exact copy of the one made by Gattemelata in 1466 for a tournament that took place in Piazza dei Signori. The nearby university is the second oldest in Italy, and it was here that Galileo taught mathematics and Goldoni took his law degree. In the neighborhood, Pedrocchi's is a favorite haunt of local intellectuals—it was also once the scene of conspiracies during the Austrian occupation. St. Anthony's Basilica is the spiritual fulcrum of a city in which Eastern elements provide contrast to the Romanesque and gothic lines which are clearly of Western inspiration.

Another city with much to offer from an artistic and cultural point of view is Verona, world renowned as the setting for the love story between Romeo and Juliet. During the summer months, an open-air representation of this famous tragedy can be seen in the Roman Theater. At the same time of year, one can listen to an opera in the spectacular setting of the Arena. A strange legend has it that the imposing amphitheater was nearly completed in a single night by the Devil himself, as he had made a pact with a wealthy local squire who had been sentenced to death for committing a serious crime. As the squire implored desperately for mercy, he was told that if he could build an enormous edifice between the Ave Maria

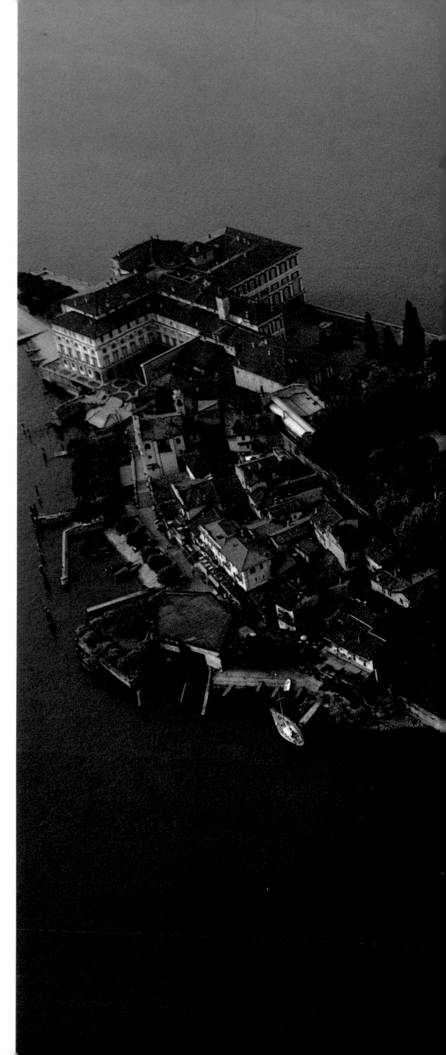

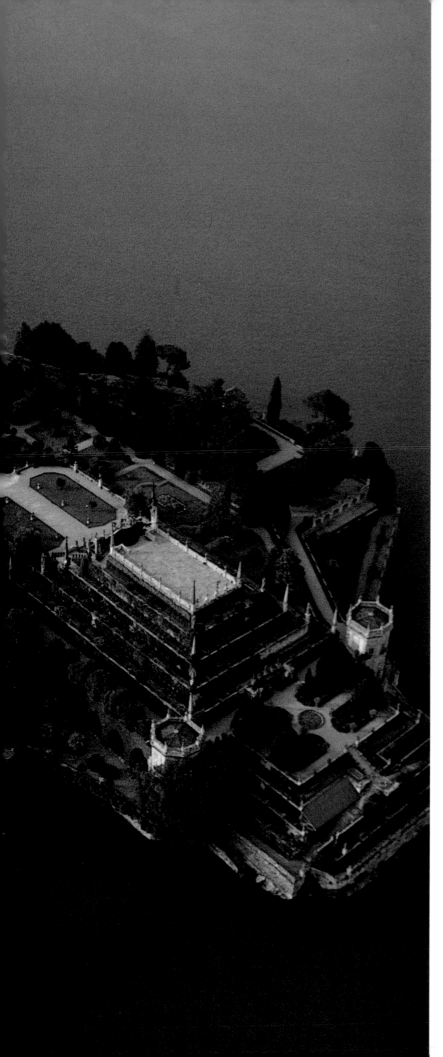

evening prayers and the following morning, his life would be saved. He had no other choice but to exchange his soul for the Devil's help. An army of demons worked all night long and the building was almost finished when the fatal hour struck. The demons returned to Hell and the Arena remained incomplete; it is easy to imagine what happened to the heartless squire. The monument remains one of the best conserved masterpieces of Roman engineering in the world, despite the fact that it was seriously ravaged during the Middle Ages.

Of a decidedly 14th-century flavor, the magnificent Piazza delle Erbe is filled with the awnings of market stalls. Going on to the nearby Piazza Dante, it is worth raising one's eyes to the Arco della Costa, which has taken its unusual name from a whale's rib that whitens as it hangs under the large supporting arch. The entire center of Verona is a maze of tiny streets and antique mansions. The city also boasts an excellent cuisine which includes some of the traditional dishes of the Veneto region such as "paperete," a type of pasta, chicken livers, and the renowned "frittura," a mixture of fried fish. Last but not least, there is the famous Pandoro cake. After satisfying the palate, the walking tour can be continued by going along the Adige, passing by the Cathedral and the superb Castelvecchio, to finally arrive in front of the splendid Romanesque Basilica dedicated to San Zeno, the city's patron saint. A visit here is not to be missed, as one of the most important paintings of the Italian Renaissance, a triptych by Mantegna, is on the high altar of this church.

Mantova, located in Lombard territory though linked to the Veneto by spirit and culture, owes its unusual aspect to the course of the Mincio River which enlarges like a lake to surround it on three sides and gives it the aspect of a lagoon. Nearby marshes and swamps are populated by thousands of wild ducks, coots, herons, and egrets: it is not at all surprising that this natural environment becomes a paradise for bird watchers from spring to late summer. Because of its natural isolation, Mantova has been able to keep its original medieval appearance as a city of art and culture. It was in the central Piazza Sordello that Petrarch received the laurel crown that made him poet laureate in 1349. The Castello di San Giorgio and the Palazzo del Te are visually stimulating constructions of undoubted charm, and the royal palace of the Gonzaga family ranks second only to the Vatican as one of the largest monumental complexes in Italy.

A little farther south, arriving in the rich, green countryside of Emilia, it is impossible to resist the call of Ferrara, whose magic dates from the Renaissance, though it still has the traces of its medieval civilization as well. Here, humanity left one of its most significant traces. The ground echoes with history. The monuments seem to reawaken the ghosts of the noble ladies and knights of whom Ariosto sang. Among the Renaissance arts encouraged by the Gonzaga, the cuisine should not be forgotten. Ferrara is highly renowned for the eels of the nearby Delta; another typical dish is "salama da sugo," which is recalled by Bacchelli in his novel *Mulino del Po.*

After one crosses the valley of Comacchio, the city of Ravenna soon becomes visible on the horizon. Today Ravenna is a few miles from the sea, but originally it was a small island at the mouth of the Po, as shown by the mausoleum of Teodorico. This city is famous for the superb mosaics which adorn the interior of monuments such as the Basilica of San Vitale, forming such a contrast with the simple, almost austere exteriors. The mortal remains of Dante are in Ravenna in a modest building which is somewhat disappointing, given the image the Italians have of this very great poet.

Leaving behind the poignant architecture of Ravenna, one arrives at the very popular beaches of Romagna, as famous for its seaside resorts as it is for the hospitality of its people and the worldliness of its numerous meeting places. From Milano Marittima to Pesaro, the coast is packed with villages and towns that are busy until dawn with a frenzied nightlife that is enjoyed by tourists and the young people who flock to its many futuristic discotheques. A bit inland, the scenic medieval village of Gradara is situated on a hill and still protected by ancient walls. This tiny center is dominated by the huge castle in whose rooms the tragic love between Paolo and Francesca da Rimini developed. Lining the steep, narrow streets are craft workshops and food shops featuring "piadina," a sandwich made with two slices of flat, unleavened bread, a delicious specialty claimed both by the Marches and Romagna.

In the hills of the Marches, travelers have the opportunity to admire the highest expression of Renaissance architecture in the town of Urbino, an almost perfectly preserved jewel dating from the 15th century. In summer, this usually quiet town is enlivened by exciting cultural, artistic, and social events which show it in all its splendor. There is still a strong attachment to the medieval past in this region, and the large number of pageants bear witness to this. A celebration that recalls former wild boar hunts takes place at Mondavio between the valleys of Metauro and Cesano, and another, the "Torneo della Quintana," takes place annually at Ascoli Piceno.

Now Umbria comes into view, a region that is rich in history and unique for its generous scenery. Its spir-

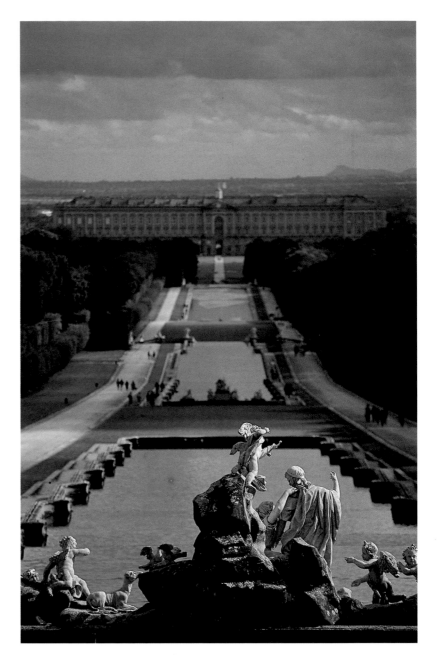

20 *The marvelous park designed by Luigi Vanvitelli for the Royal Palace at Caserta stretches for nearly a mile with spectacular effect, incorporating pools, fountains, and artificial waterfalls.*

21 top *A group of statues representing the myth of Actaeon decorates one side of the Grande Cascata, or large waterfall, in the gardens of the Royal Palace at Caserta.*

21 bottom *Built on the orders of the Bourbon King Carlo, the Royal Palace of Caserta soon became known as the "Italian Versailles" because of its massive scale and grand perspectives.*

22 top *Saint Mark's Basilica is the pride of Venice. Above the doorways, semicircular lunettes frame colorful mosaics in intricate mouldings.*

22 center *The Doge's Palace, magnificent residence of the Venetian rulers, is a testament to the power and splendor of the old Venetian Republic.*

22 bottom *Saint Andrea's Basilica is the main monument in the city of Vercelli, and one of the earliest examples of gothic architecture in Italy.*

23 *With a solemn, three-naved interior and a polygonal cupola, Parma Cathedral is one of the best surviving examples of Italian Romanesque architecture.*

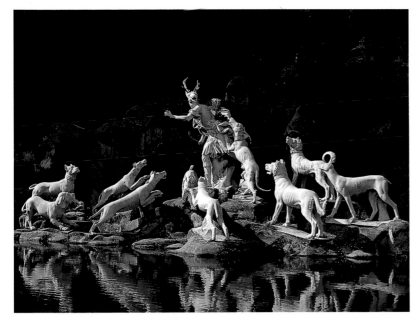

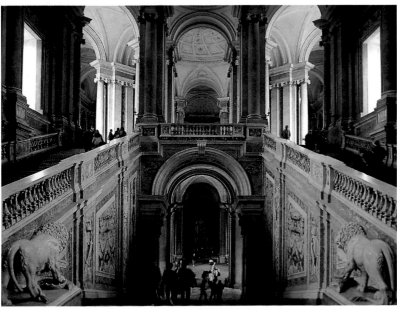

itual capital is without doubt Assisi, and its Basilica is dedicated to Saint Francis. This is truly the heritage of the whole of humanity, built with generous donations sent from all the countries of the world. The church is subdivided into two parts. The saint's tomb is in the lower part, framed by frescoes painted by Cimabue, while the upper church is renowned for the 28 frescoes which Giotto painted to illustrate the life of Saint Francis. The small medieval houses, the numerous holy buildings, the noble mansions, and the craftsmen's workshops one encounters along the way render even more precious the mystical setting of these remains.

Nearby is the small town of Deruta, which is world renowned for the production of artistic ceramics which flourished particularly in the 16th century. In September at Foligno, it is well worthwhile to see the renowned Quintana tournament. During this exhibition, men galloping on horseback at a furious pace try to remove with their lances the ring that hangs from the arm of a wooden statue of a Moor in the center of the arena.

Crossing the land of Abruzzo, whose magnificent natural beauty reaches its high point in the Abruzzo National Park, it is still possible to observe the brown marsican bear in its natural habitat. At this point, one returns to the Adriatic coast at the point where the headland of Gargano juts out into the sea. The green, gnarled, Aleppo pines that descend toward the sea are perched on the steep white cliffs, hiding the little pebbly beaches that can often be reached only by water. The people here speak such a broad dialect that other inhabitants of this region who wish to describe someone who speaks in an incomprehensible way say that he is a "giargianese," or a person from Gargano.

The Tremiti Islands, whose steep coasts are surrounded by an eternally blue sea, can be seen from these golden sandy beaches. Proceeding along this splendid coast, perhaps stopping off at Manfredonia to enjoy a tasty dish of spaghetti with mussels and other seafood specialties, we soon reach Bari, one of the most active towns of the Apulian region. Without doubt the most interesting part is the old section of the town from which emerges the Basilica di San Nicola. Its austere facade makes it one of the most majestic churches in southern Italy.

An unforgettable itinerary takes us down to Taranto via Castellana, renowned for the mysterious caves discovered there in 1938. We then continue through Alberobello, a small village with characteristic, cone-shaped houses known as "trulli" before finally arriving in sunny Locorotondo, where one can quench a parching thirst with a glass of good local wine. Like Bari, Taranto is divided into two distinct zones. There is an old part, a tiny, charming isle surrounded on the opposite bank by a more modern zone. In these districts some streets are so narrow that only two people can walk along them side by side: the narrow paths were a form of defense from the periodical Moorish invasions. In the fisherman's quarter there are many stalls where passers-by can buy freshly caught seafood. If one is lucky and patient, one can see the ceremony in which the ships of the Italian Navy enter the so-called Mar Piccolo (the small sea) by way of the swing bridge which unites the old and new parts of the city.

On your journey, take advantage of the beautiful beaches that face the Gulf and relax in the hot sun. For people who like rugged walks, this area, especially where it borders on Basilicata, offers interesting walks across the Murge, calcareous mountains and gullies hollowed out by rainwater. Remains of ancient homes, caves, and churches dug out of stone in the Middle Ages are hidden between these gullies. An almost intact example of the successive developments undergone by these dwellings can be found in the Sassi di Matera.

Here it is interesting to climb up the steep, narrow streets and go into the houses or the local shops. In this archaic setting, classic films such as "La Lupa" and "Cristo si é fermato ad Eboli" (Christ stopped at Eboli) were made. This rugged and undulating scenery continues into the region of Calabria, a land of great contrasts, with green pine trees covering the Sila mountains and typical Mediterranean vegetation on the coast. Near Catanzaro there are still communities which hand down from father to son the traditions and language of their Albanese forefathers who arrived in the 15th century during the Aragonese domination. On clear days, both seas can be seen from high points, and in ancient times there was a great deal of commercial traffic on these waters. This area has always been plagued by strong winds and impetuous sea currents, and it was these which gave rise to the myth of Scylla and Charybdis, the terrible sea monsters who were supposedly responsible for so many shipwrecks in ancient times. In recent years spectacular archeological finds have been made, the most important of which are the very famous bronzes of Riace now kept in Reggio di Calabria. With modern navigation techniques, crossing the straits is no longer a problem. Indeed, it is worth taking a ferry to enjoy the magnificent view one has approaching this island that, according to Homer, was inhabited by Cyclops. This region is mainly mountainous, and its highest point is the massive Etna volcano. One has the best view of this mountain from Taormina and from the ruins of the great Greek-Roman theater to which Etna provides a permanent backdrop. On this histori-

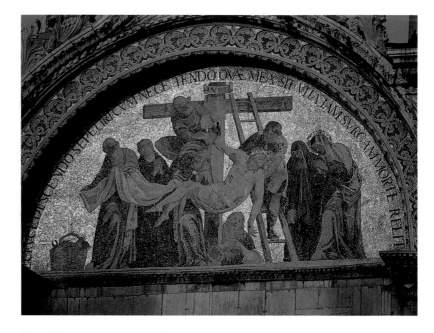

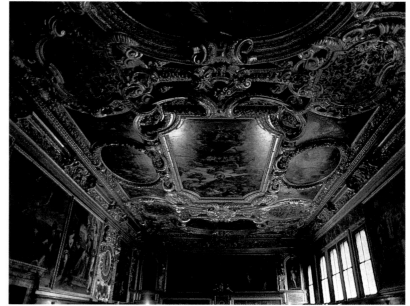

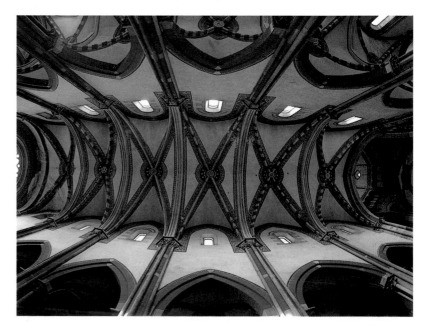

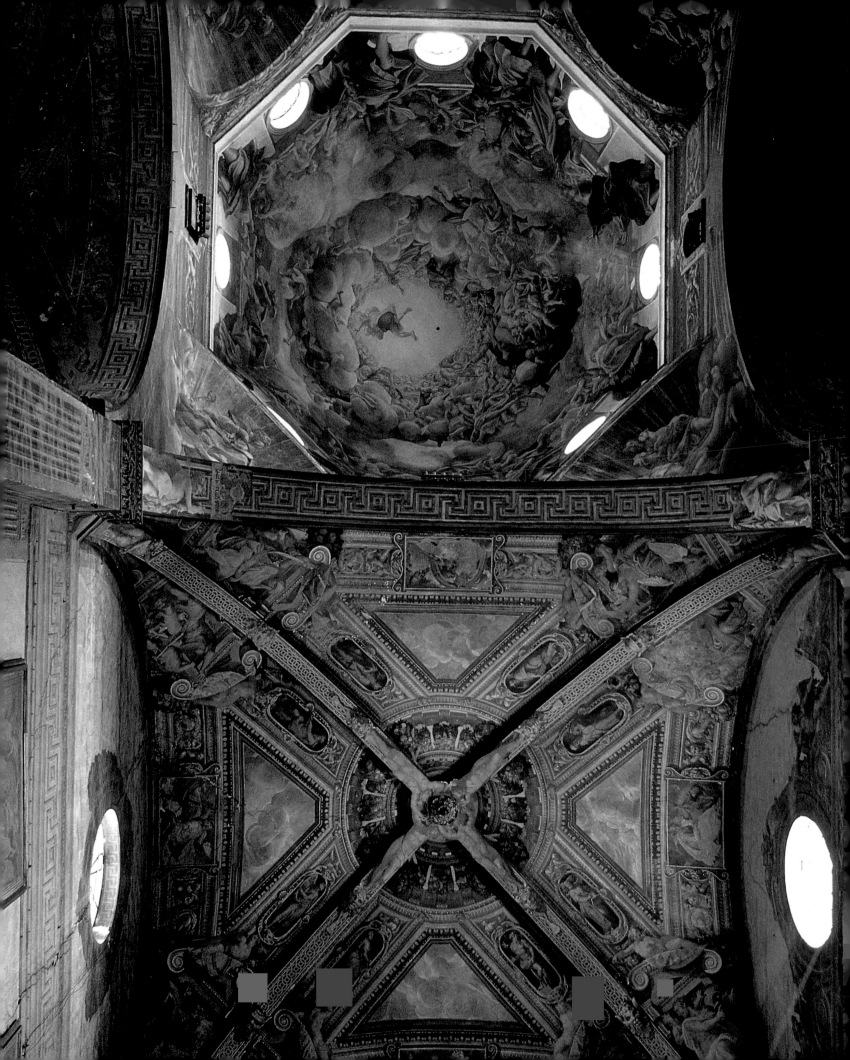

cal stage, the tragedies of the great Greek authors are still played, sometimes in the original language, and they are even more intense because of the marvelous scenery. Between these parched horizons it becomes clear that Sicily's most original attraction is its animated history and its uncountable monuments that bear witness to the continuous presence of foreigners.

Palermo is an impressive city because of the architectural styles left by Phoenicians, Greeks, Carthaginians, Romans, Normans, French, and finally Spanish. Piazza dei Quattro Canti, surrounded by the facades of beautiful Baroque mansions, is a very good starting point from which to begin a walk around the city. From here, it is easy to get to the sumptuous cathedral, which was begun in the 12th century and which contains the tombs of the Norman kings in an almost fairy tale setting. The Cappella Palatina is another treasure chest which sums up the highest expression of three civilizations: Byzantine, Arab, and Norman. As one walks around the center, which is dotted with palm trees and exotic plants, one unexpectedly comes across Arab domes or the Baroque forms of tumble-down mansions, and one begins to understand the chaotic spirit and soul of the Sicilian people.

A ferry trip from the busy port of Palermo brings us to Sardinia, Italy's other big island which has a very particular history of its own. This mountainous island offers some of the most spectacularly beautiful scenery in the entire country. Its morphology ruggedly highlights the difference between the plains, the mountains, and the plateaus where there are few villages and where resides the island's most ancient soul. Even the coasts, despite an illusion of uniformity, have a great variety of shapes, and many beaches, coves, and spectacular rock formations alternate with each to form the most evocative of natural landscapes. The transparent emerald green water and the distinctive pink sands are a permanent invitation to do nothing but enjoy oneself. In the background, the historical and artistic heritage of this region is different from that of any other part of the nation. One cannot ignore the presence of the "nuraghi," the megalithic, cone-shaped constructions built with enormous stones, or the presence of the even more mysterious "Domus de Janas," small rooms without windows which were dug out of the rock and which have fostered the belief that, in ancient times, Sardinia was inhabited by gnomes. The older part of the island's capital, Cagliari, is built on a high hill dominated by the castle and towers. Around this the more modern quarters have been built, descending gradually towards the sea, and its wharves where the intense activity that characterizes the biggest port of this part of the Mediterranean is carried out. Opening out onto this industrious stretch of

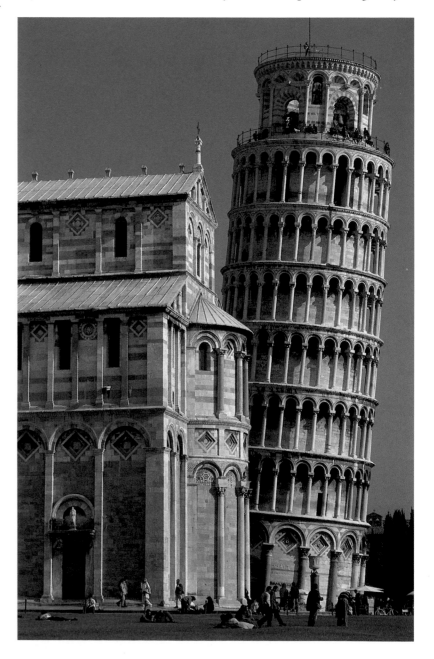

24 *One of the world's most famous towers because of its proportions and its inclination, the Tower of Pisa is said to have been the testing ground for Galileo's experiments on gravity.*

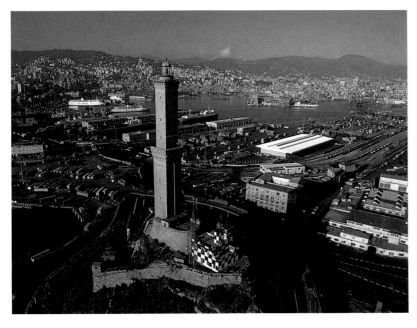

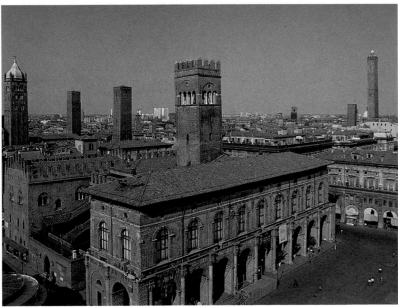

water is the wide and elegant Via Roma, the center of the town which is always animated by evening strollers. Roads go off from here and climb gently up the hill, and this is where one can admire precious and solemn traces of the past that have remained intact despite the extensive development of this metropolis.

Heading back to the "continent," (Sardinians always call Italy "il continente") by air or by sea, we now reach Naples. Arriving by sea, and after passing the Isle of Capri which, until a few years ago, was highly popular with American tourists, and catching a distant glimpse of the lovely island of Ischia, the city of Naples comes into view with its houses built in terraces on the surrounding hills. Everything is dominated by the threatening form of Vesuvius. This chaotic and vital city represents the unruly side of Italy for many people. The sun, the tarantella, and the philosophy of living day by day have always been considered, perhaps rightly, to sum up the people of Naples. Everyday life can be observed by exploring the busy streets in the old part of the city where confusion reigns, where entire families live in so-called "bassi," small, narrow rooms on the ground level, and where most of the daily work is carried out in the streets. It is this exuberance that gives Naples its charm, as do its street festivals and popular traditions including the famous Neapolitan song festival, founded in honor of the Madonna di Piedigrotta, or the celebration of the miracle of the liquifaction of San Gennaro's blood. San Gennaro is the city's patron saint, and it is said that the luck of the city depends on this miracle for the following year. (It is considered to be a bad sign if the blood does not liquefy.)

Numerous monuments bear witness to a glorious past and keep alive the memories of the city's history. The imposing Maschio Angioino still seems to protect the entrance to the port, whereas in the Cappella Sansevero the two statues of Disinganno and Pudicizia (Disenchantment and Modesty) continue to amaze us with their unparalleled technical virtuosity. This building holds many legends as mysterious as the existence of the patrician who built it as his tomb in the 18th century. One could say that there is a particular myth linked to each corner of the city. In addition to all the other claims the city can make, it is also known as the unrivaled queen of the pizza. This popular dish is prepared in many different forms, ranging from the classical round to the so-called pizza "a metro" (by the meter) which one can buy in slices.

From the summit of Vesuvius, one can contemplate the plain that was once the site of Pompei and Herculaneum, the two Roman cities buried by the eruption in 79 B.C. Archeological excavations, which have lasted more than a century, have provided us with a description of daily life 2,000 years ago. There are other surprises to be discovered along the Amalfi coast, the superb, natural paradise along which precipices and vertiginous cliffs open onto a crystal clear sea. The area of Circeo to the north is also renowned for its beaches and the pretty sea villages that compete with each other for wonderful scenery. The entire area, as far as Fregene and beyond, has been a favorite spot for spending the summer months ever since the days of the Roman Empire.

Today this coast is still crowded with inhabitants of the capital who, in their free time, prefer to flee the chaotic metropolis in which they live. Despite the easy-going mentality of its people, Rome is a city in continual movement, partly because of the thousands of tourists that invade it every day. It is amazing to see how the traffic manages to get around the innumerable vestiges of the past, from the Colosseum to Piazza Venezia, from Castel Sant'Angelo to Trinità dei Monti, with such nonchalance. Romans still take pride in the traditions of Rome as "caput mundi." Their pride is fully justified by the magnificence of this city. Walking through the Fori Imperiali, one is reminded of the ancient pomp. Along the narrow streets of Trastevere, you can easily forget that this is in the capital because this area gives the impression of being in a small village of old Lazio with children playing ball and gossips chatting at the windows. In the center between Piazza Navona and the Trevi Fountain, there are also very quiet streets onto which face picturesque restaurants where one must taste the wine from the Castelli Romani, or the lesser known "fragolino" wine. Observing the famous Bocca della Verita, the Roman mask that according to tradition cuts the hand off anyone who tells lies, it is strange to think that Rome is the bureaucratic city par excellence, heart of the animated and often contradictory political life of the country. Equally important decisions are made in the heart of the Eternal City, in the tiny but extremely powerful Vatican State which is the seat of the Pontiff. Saint Peter's Basilica, surmounted by Michelangelo's dome, is the symbol of Christianity, whereas the nearby Vatican Museums contain some of mankind's greatest cultural heritage.

Siena is a close relation to Rome, at least according to a legend that says is was founded by Senio, the son of Remo. This city also has a particular charm and is very pleasant to tour on foot, especially during the colorful and exciting Palio, a horse race run on July 2nd and August 16th every year. On this occasion, the entire city lets itself go with uncontrollable merrymaking that involves each of the 17 districts. The incredible horse race takes place after a sumptuous procession in Renaissance costumes, including a performance by

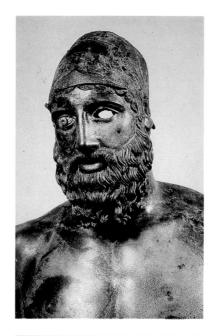

26-27 *Masterpieces of Greek sculpture dating from the 5th century B.C., the bronze statues of Riace spent more than 2,000 years at the bottom of the Ionic Sea before they were discovered accidentally by a fisherman in 1972. It is thought that these two enormous bronze statues of warriors were lost during a storm on a voyage between Calabria and Greece. They are now the principal attraction in the Museo Nazionale della Magna Grecia in Reggio di Calabria.*

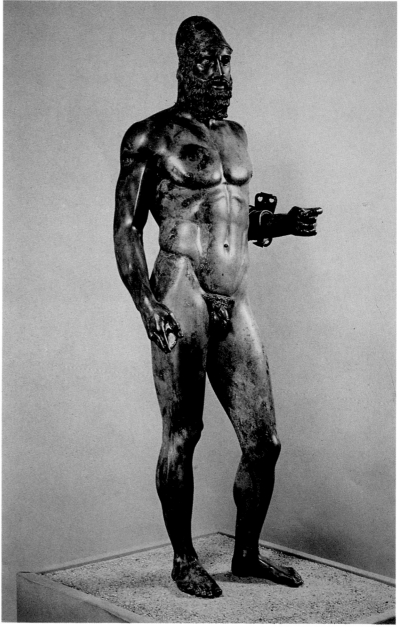

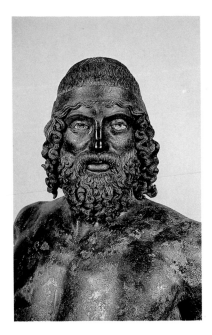

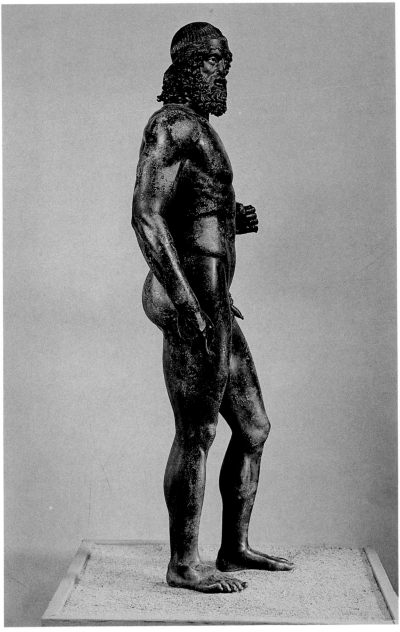

the famous flag wavers.

Florence, too, has its own charm, due to the medieval and Renaissance architecture within the perimeter of the old walls which give a proud and elegant character to the city. The inhabitants are austere and critical but can also be brilliant and possess a pungent wit. The historical center between the Cathedral, Palazzo Vecchio, and Palazzo Strozzi is still the throbbing heart of city life, enlivened by a cosmopolitan crowd. The shops in Via Calzaiuoli, Via Roma, and Via Tornabuoni are the most elegant and exclusive, as are the numerous meeting places that can also be found there. The glittering shop windows are in strong contrast with the nearby Mercato della Paglia, where one can find all sorts of curiosities including objects made with the famous red Florentine leather, or in May, tiny cages containing chirping grasshoppers. From the panoramic Piazzale Michelangelo, one's gaze can stretch beyond Brunelleschi's cupola and Giotto's bell tower to embrace the rolling hills which surround the city. Florence has managed to conserve an extensive green setting around the city center.

Passing fields divided by rows of cypresses in the countryside around Fiesole and proceeding through the Tusco-Emilian Apennine forests, we reach the Po plain, which is announced by the opulent city of Bologna. This city is universally known as the "dotta," (cultured) and the "grassa," (fat). The first of these nicknames is due to its long cultural tradition; it was here at the beginning of the 13th century that Europe's oldest university was founded. The second nickname is derived from the worldwide fame of the local gastronomy. Tortellini, tagliatelle, suckling pig, and good wine explain why it is common to think of the Bolognese woman as being beautiful and glowing with health. From the height of its towers, of which the Asinelli and Garisenda are the most famous, one can enjoy the characteristic panorama enhanced by the red city roofs. A walk along the arcades of this regional capital helps one understand the Bolognese spirit and the openness and hospitality of her people.

Unlike Bologna, Genoa appears prouder and more closed, almost as if its inhabitants still had the instinct to fight for independence; or perhaps this is due to the fact that this city is not only the biggest port in Italy but also a large industrial center. Despite its fame as a commercial town, Genoa is above all a beautiful city. Because of the majestic way in which the buildings are built down toward the sea and the haughtiness of its monuments, it is known as "La Superba," or "the arrogant." Its beauty lies in the contrast between old and new: in streets that have a quiet, aristocratic air about them, in the tangle of "caruggi" (lanes) full of

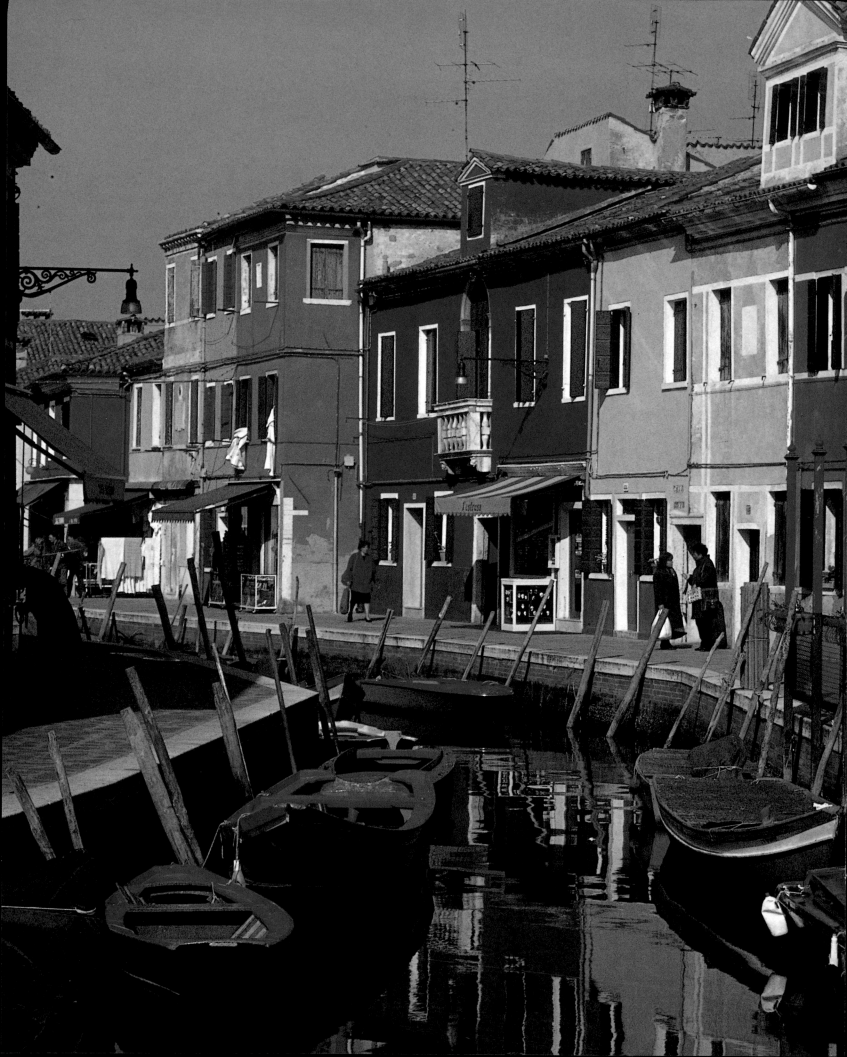

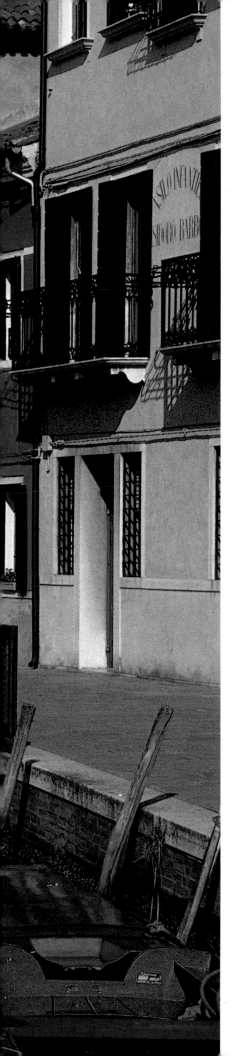

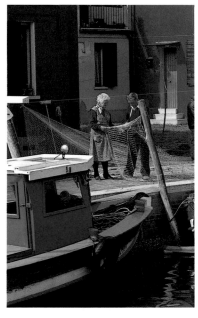

28-29 *Colorful houses line the waterfront in Burano, a characteristic fishing village built on four small islets in the Venetian Lagoon. Burano is crisscrossed by many navigable canals. The village is known for its lace-making, a skill which has flourished here since the Middle Ages.*

30-31 *Fashion critics gather from all parts of the world to attend the fashion shows in Milan, famous for their style and elegance.*

confusion and agitation, and in the glimpses of the panorama that can be caught of the hinterland or the seaside.

The fact that tasty "pesto" was invented here as well as many other dishes and delicacies distracts us from the fact that the Genovese are known for their avarice; on the other hand, the fact that their region principally consists of an arc of mountains and steep hills, which means that their only resources could come from a narrow strip of arable land and from the sea, might help to justify this reputation. The Ligurian scenery is varied, as is that of the entire territory of the region. Genoa is in the center of the arc. To the East is the Riviera di Levante, inaccessible because of its rocky, high, steep coasts with small, deep inlets and coves enclosed between narrow headlands. The villages that give the name Cinque Terre to the area seem to have been wedged by force between the cliffs and the sea, and have kept a good deal of their old charm. There are tiny creeks and coves on the headland of Portofino where the sea, rocks, greenery, and animal life are wonderful to see. To the West of Genoa is the Riviera di Ponente, also called the Riviera dei Fiori because of the cultivation of flowers on the hills overlooking the sea. This coast is less harsh, with gentler reliefs and shallower inlets where sandy beaches form one of the world's best-known tourist attractions.

Beyond the Northern Apennines, the much richer land of Piedmont in the zones known as Langhe, Asti, and Monferrato is famous for the beauty of its scenery and even more so for its excellent wines. This is the more intimate, secluded Piedmont that even people who live in the same region do not know. Here each tiny village has its own history, which can be deduced by the presence of numerous castles or the votive pictures in the numerous chapels in the country.

Leaving these magnificent hills and following in the footsteps of the many people who have preferred to abandon hard work in the fields, one arrives in Turin, an elegant and slightly old-fashioned city. "Piedmontese falso e cortese," "false but polite" says the proverb, and it is perhaps true. Turin is symbolic of this region and presents itself as a distinguished, refined, and snobbish city. Toward the outskirts it is possible to see the signs of the formidable economic power that has been developed by heavy industry during this century. A temple to the latter is the Automobile Museum, where its history is well illustrated. Turin can boast a unique urban layout with straight, tree-lined boulevards and vast scenic settings such as that of Piazza San Carlo, which everyone considers to be the city's salon. Of the many museums the most important is the Egyptian museum, which is second in size only to the one in Cairo. The records of the long fight for Italian unity are added to the already remarkable cultural attractions of the city. Quite visible from the top of the Mole Antonelliana or the Superga hill, the Valle d'Aosta opens on the horizon, with the unmistakable form of the Serra of Ivrea in the foreground, an immense glacial moraine formed in prehistoric times.

In the midst of Europe's highest mountains, among which the imposing massif of Monte Bianco stands out, the Valle d'Aosta is dominated by the immense expanse of Monte Rosa, a gigantic stone sentinel which forms the border with Switzerland. It is indeed a unique spectacle. The Alpine panorama is characterized by the jagged contours of the highest peaks and the imposing walls of granite whose dominating colors range from the grey to the white of the eternal snow, softened in summer by the intense green of the pine forests. The Gran Paradiso National Park, situated in this spectacular area, is the largest and most important in Italy. Here it is possible to see ibex and chamois climbing up the steep paths and the grassy slopes of the mountain. There is a very strong Francophone tradition in this region, easily deduced from the dialect and the local place names. The area is dotted with numerous manors overlooking the road that leads to Aosta, a town that was founded by Julius Caesar's legionnaires and that is among the best preserved of the Roman Empire. Many of the villages that are nestled in the valley have been transformed into well-equipped skiing resorts in the last 30 years, and they attract crowds in all seasons because of the wonderful scenery and folklore traditions. Among the many valleys, each one leading to a spectacular group of mountains, the Valtournanche has the Matterhorn, which is second only to the majestic Monte Bianco. The harsh grey of these granite massifs, covered with permanent glaciers, is completely different from the warm rosy shade of Dolomitic limestone which is the fortune and glory of the Cime di Lavaredo and other numerous peaks at the eastern end of the Alpine arc, one of the major Italian destinations for mountaineers.

The Dolomites have their own unmistakable personality: there are no two peaks equal in shape, appearance, or legend, or that present the same consistency to the climber's hand. Massive towers with sheer walls, minutely indented crests, and sharply pointed mountain crests rise from the vast meadows at their feet. The rocks that are generally of a reddish color take on pink, red, and violet hues at dawn and dusk. They shine from on high when the valleys are in the shade. This is why the Dolomites are one of the most popular destinations for international tourism. With spectacular peaks, large conifer woods, and small

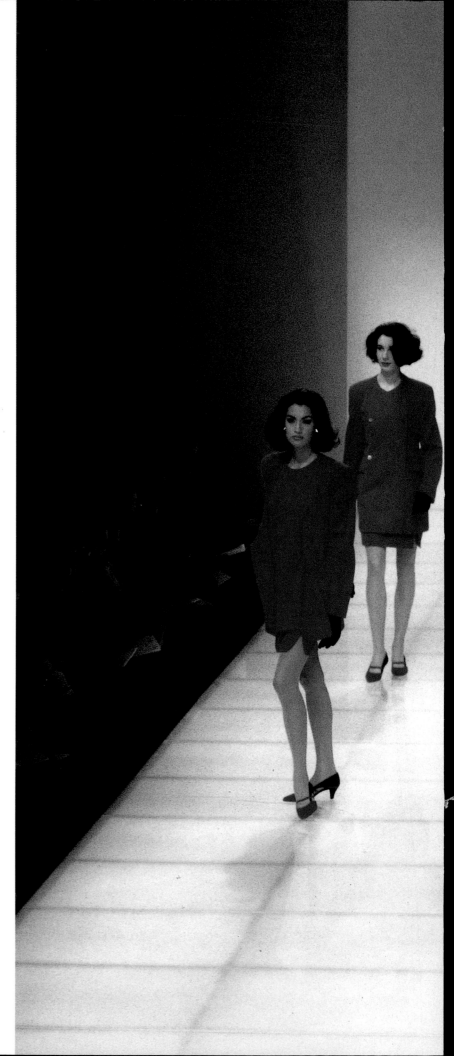

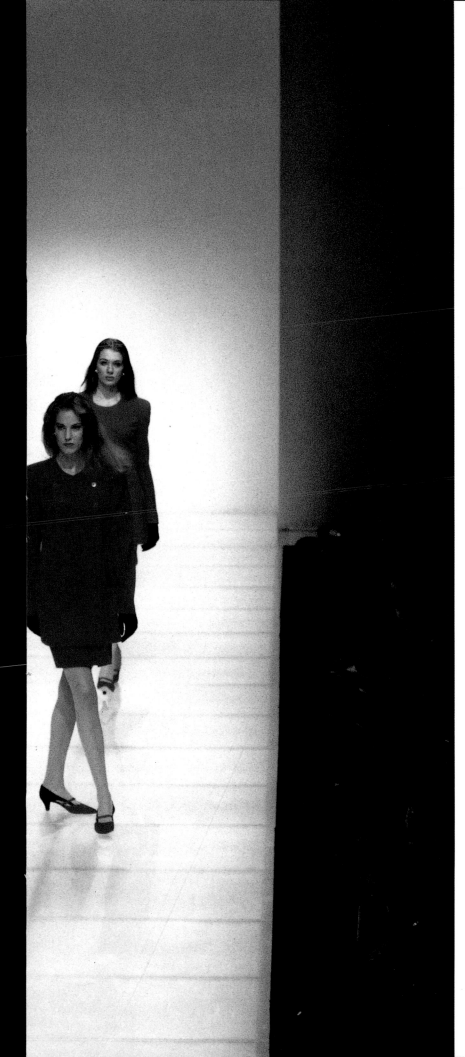

blue lakes framed by dark forests, this region is ideal for holidays, winter sports, and mountaineering. There are many tourist centers, such as Cortina d'Ampezzo, Merano, Ortisei, and Pieve di Cadore that are favorite destinations for the Milanese who, after a long week spent amidst the skyscrapers of the city, take refuge in the equally high but more relaxing scenery of Trentino.

Despite common belief, Milan is not just an enormous city strangled by traffic and smog where all the contradictions of a consumer civilization are to be found. To those who know how to appreciate it, the capital of Lombardy can offer the unusual poetry of Navigli, the brio of the "Senigallia," (flea market), and the old-fashioned romanticism of Brera. The effervescence of the city is obvious to one who walks along the central streets or who stops off in Piazza del Duomo to watch the multicolored, heterogeneous crowd bustling by. Going through the most elegant quarters such as the area in Via della Spighe or Via Montenapoleone, one can sense the snobbish love for beautiful things that has made Milan the center of refined Italian fashion which is envied by everyone. To get to know the real Milanese, take a walk in Galleria at aperitif time, or sip a coffee on the panoramic terrace of the Rinascente department store. Enjoy the unexpected peace of the streets of old Milan or, near Sant'Ambrogio, the domain of antique dealers. In Sant'Ambrogio the annual fair of "O bei O bei" is held on December 7, the patron saint's feast day, and on the same day the lyrical season begins at the Scala, perhaps the most famous opera theater in the world because of the perfection of its performances and the dedication of the musicians and singers.

Italy is all of this and still more. Through 3,000 years of history, the nation has served as a center for art and human events and the culture of the Western world. While conscious of the wealth of their past, the Italian people have kept their eternally youthful spirit and their love for life. Discrediting the clichés that once described it as a sluggish and indifferent nation, modern Italy is an important economic power and very much a presence on the international scene.

# Pride in the Past and the Future

To speak of Italian cities is to speak of art, history, culture, and life in a delicate equilibrium that is constantly renewed. Each city sums up the charm of the past through its buildings and monuments and the perpetual motion of everyday life.

The different styles of the various epochs can be seen in the architectural forms of every building or monument, street or square. But the history is not only to be found in architecture—the histories of cities are always written by their inhabitants. Generous or genial, reserved or spontaneous, the people are really what make each city unique.

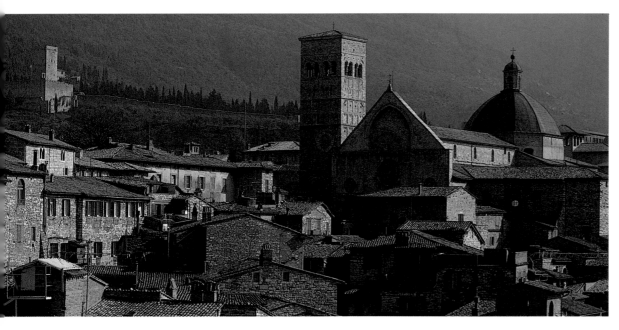

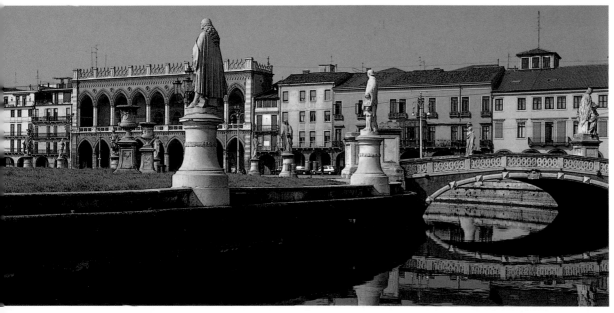

32 top *Best known as the birthplace of St. Francis, Assisi is still characterized by its narrow, winding streets and its medieval art. Despite the pressures of tourism, the city retains much of its original character.*

32 bottom *Surrounded by a canal in the center of Padua, the Prato della Valle contains a number of statues of famous citizens.*

33 *The Basilica of San Vitale in Ravenna is one of the purest creations of paleo-Christian art in Italy. The interior is decorated with splendid Byzantine mosaics of scenes taken from the Old Testament and the processions of Emperor Justinian and the Empress Theodora.*

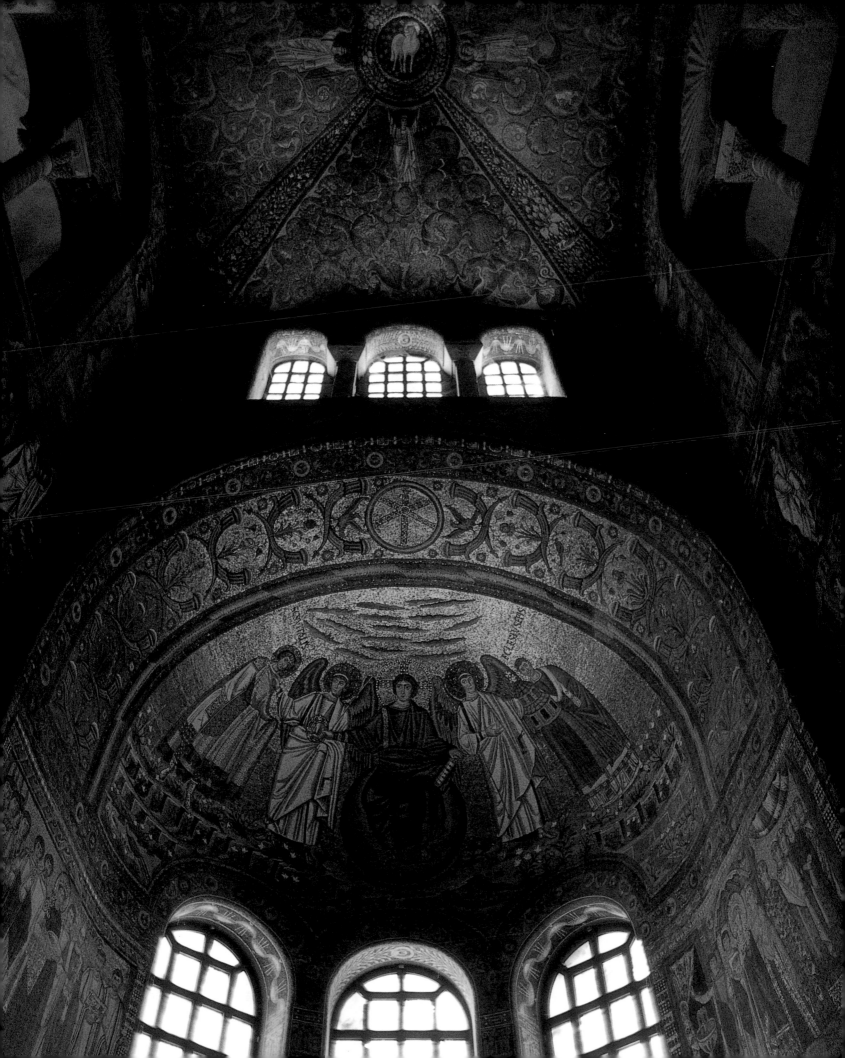

# Rome:
# A Monument to Itself

There is probably no other city in the world which can rival Rome in the solemn and magnificent traditions it has carried on through the course of time. The history of Rome embraces the history of the ancient world and of the spiritual and temporal power of the Papacy. Its destiny as capital gives it a monumental scale, spread out over seven hills.

This immense city combines its two very different natures with apparent naturalness: on the one hand, the bureaucratic officialdom which emanates from the seats of political and religious power, on the other hand, a desire for the enjoyment of life and the exuberance of its more popular quarters.

*34 left From Pincian Hill there is a splendid view of the Altare della Patria and the tomb of the unknown soldier.*

*34 top right Giovanni Lorenzo Bernini designed the angel statues that embellish Ponte Sant'Angelo.*

*34 bottom right The statues of the Dioscuri stand at the center of Piazza del Quirinale on the highest of the seven hills of Rome.*

*35 The Trevi Fountain was immortalized in Fellini's film "La Dolce Vita."*

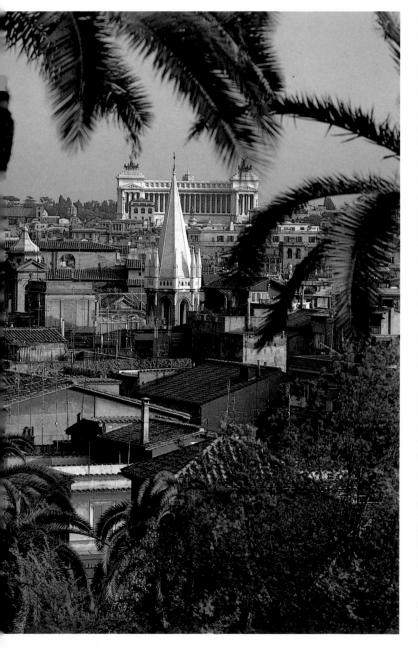

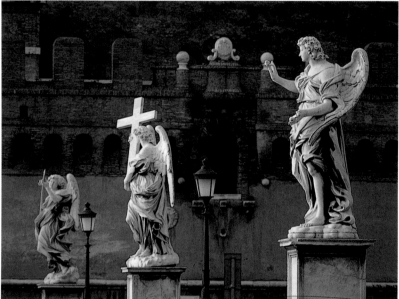

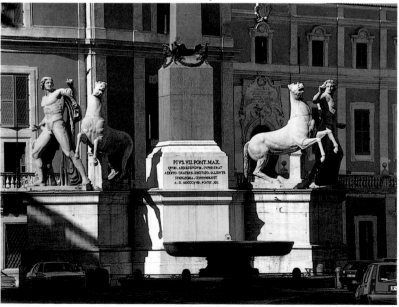

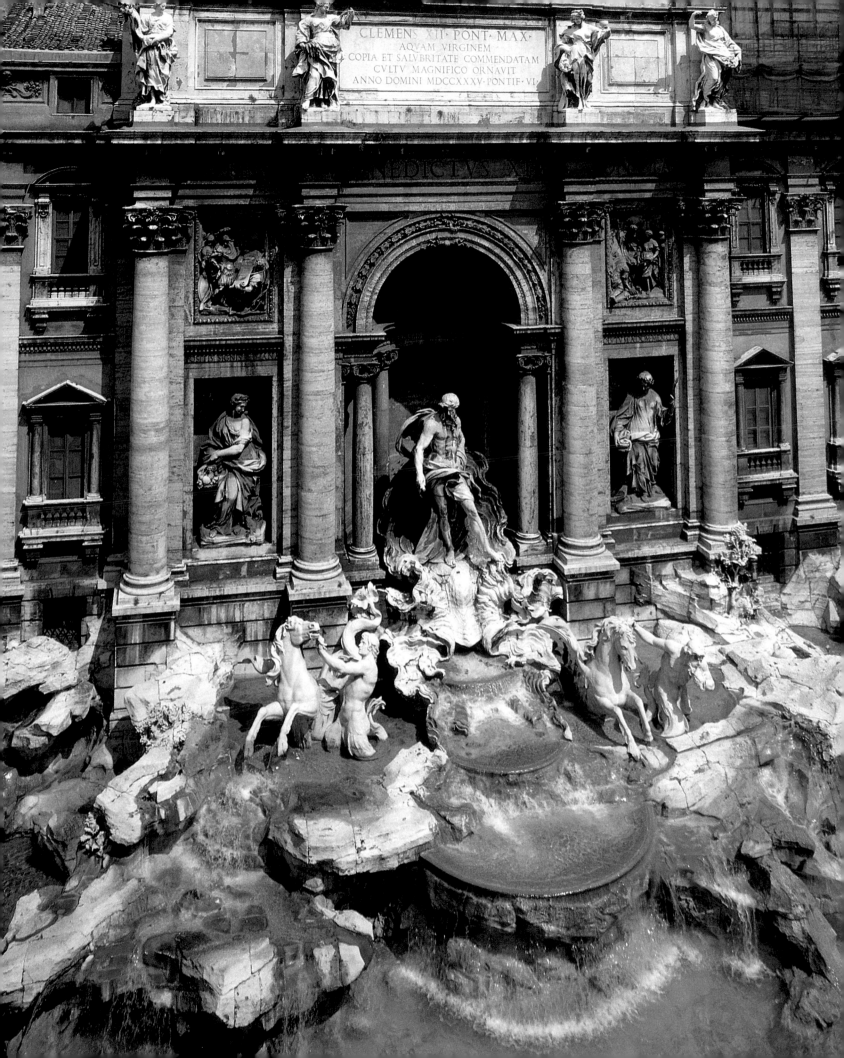

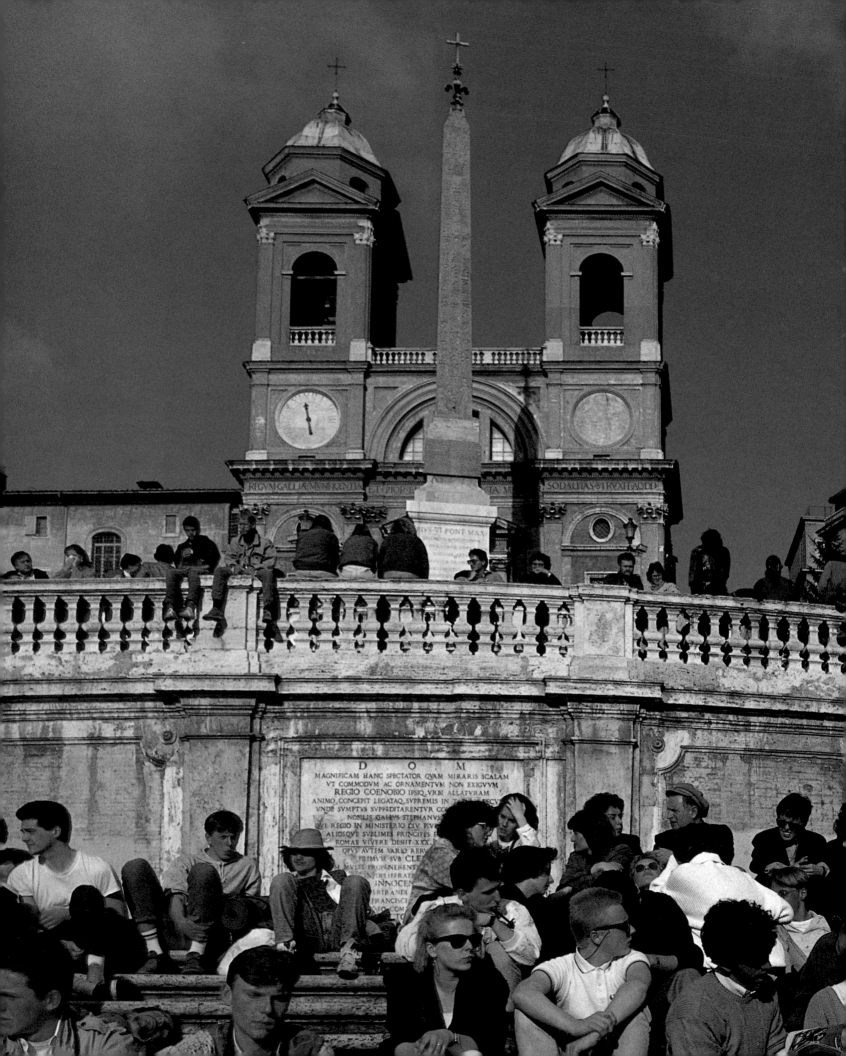

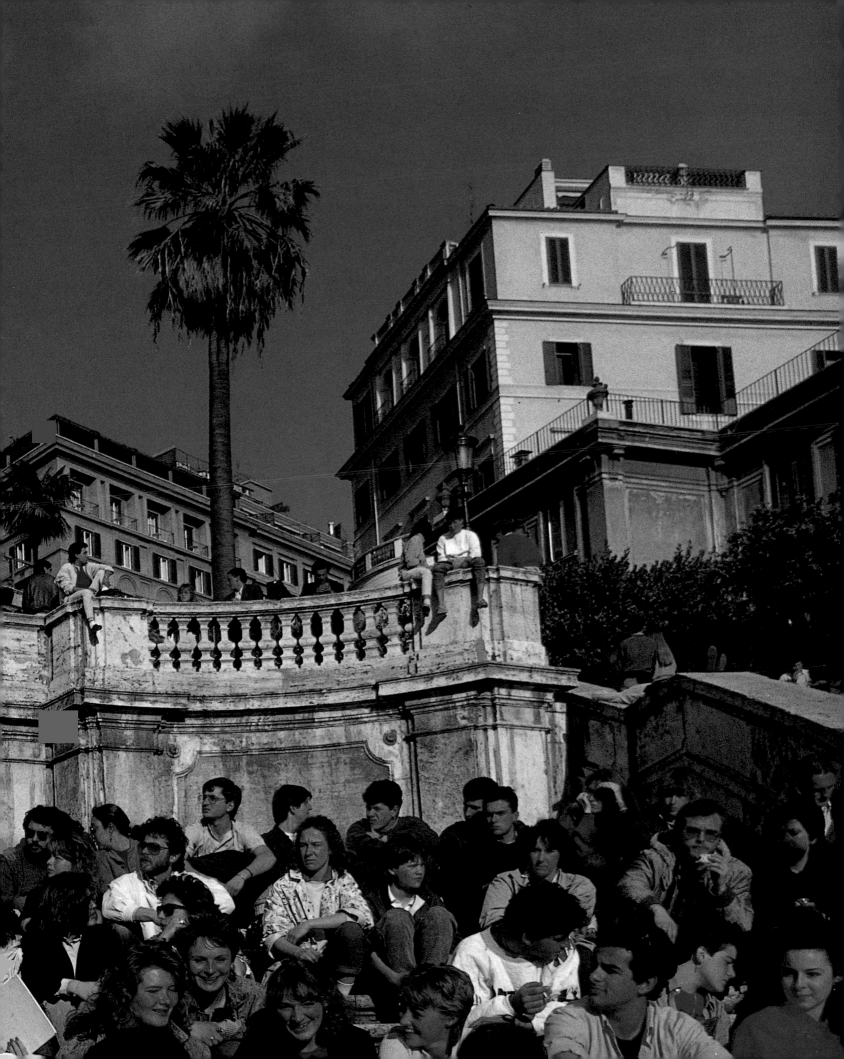

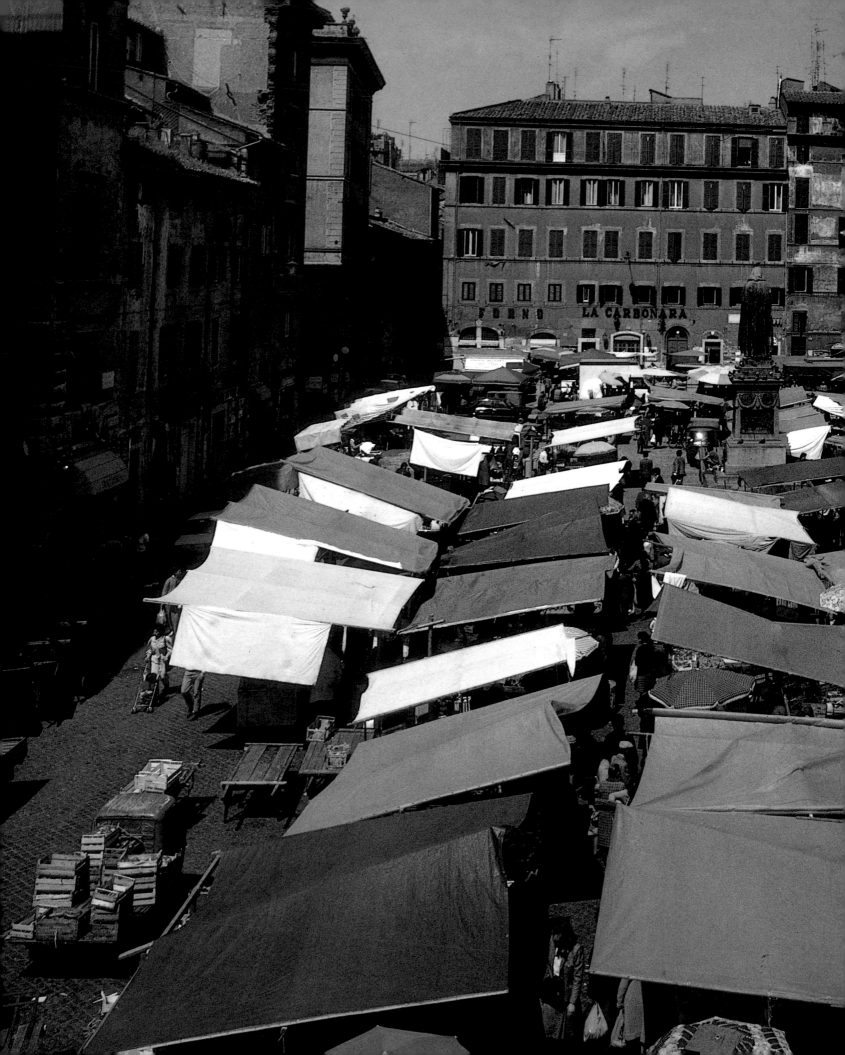

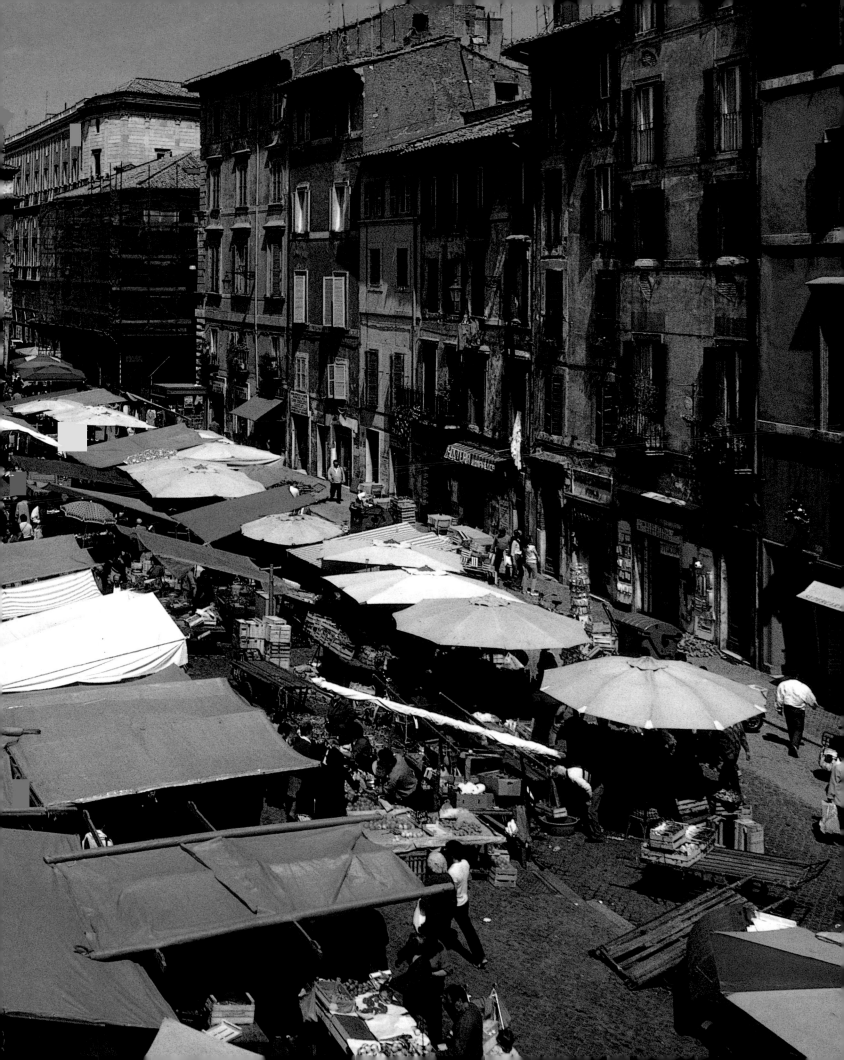

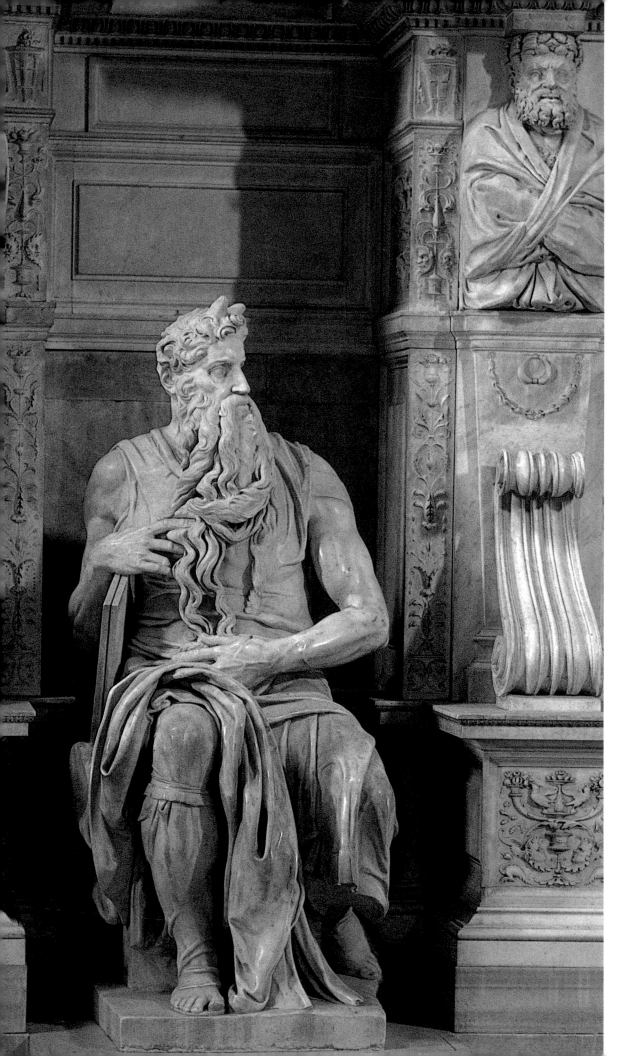

36-37 The Trinity Staircase, also known as the Spanish Steps, is one of the most frequented meeting places in the capital.

38-39 Rising above the stalls in Piazza Campo de'Fiori is the monument to Giordano Bruno, who was burned at the stake for heresy on this spot in 1600.

40 Inside the church of San Pietro in Vincoli is a mausoleum which Pope Julius II commissioned Michelangelo to build for him. The tomb was never completed. Of the statues the artist designed and sculpted for it, the only one remaining is the statue of Moses. Vasari, an artist and biographer of the period, wrote than no other sculpture, either past or future, would ever be able to equal it.

41 Heart of the Catholic world and tangible emblem of Christianity, St. Peter's Basilica contains inestimable art treasures, including Michelangelo's Pietà. The statue of the Virgin holding Christ expresses grief and regret with a touching sensitivity. A subtle sense of movement pervades the composition.

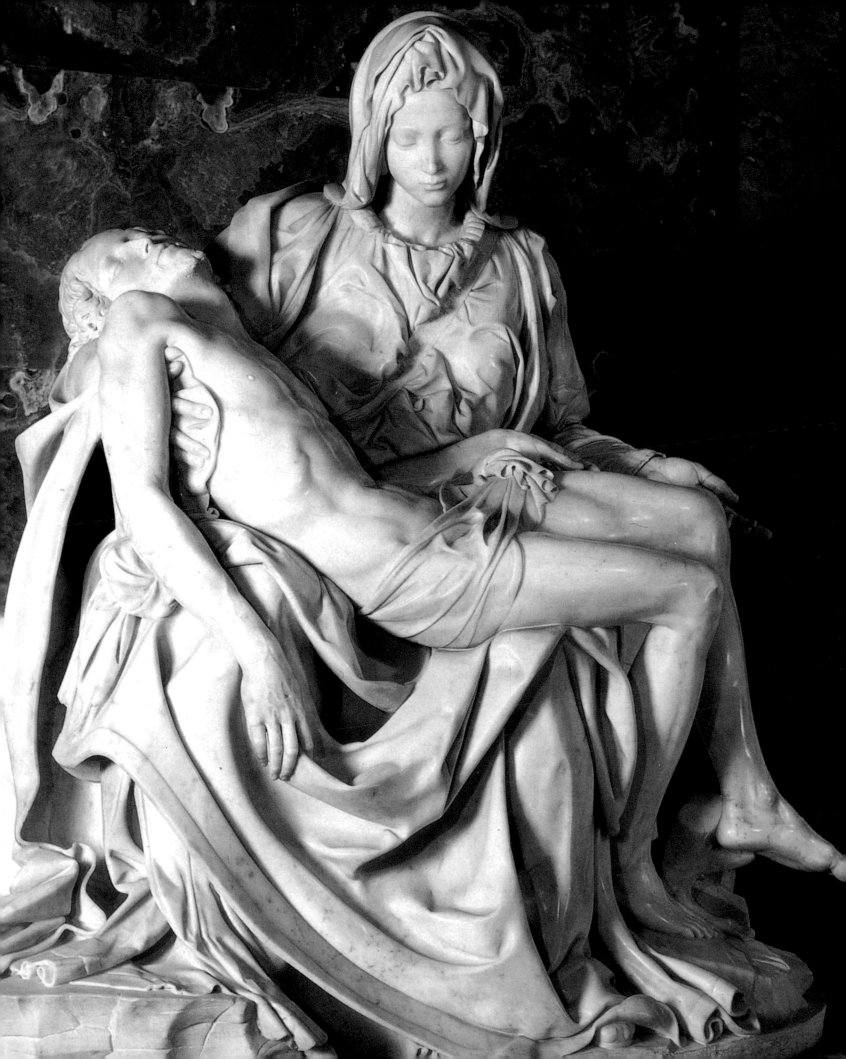

42 top *The celebrations of Holy Mass in St. Peter's Basilica always draw large crowds. The church alone can accommodate almost 60,000 people.*

42 bottom *A Swiss guard dressed in his characteristic orange-and blue-striped uniform stands at his post in front of the colonnade of St. Peter's Square, Bernini's masterpiece.*

42-43 *Each Sunday, thousands of the faithful gather in the Square to listen to the Pope.*

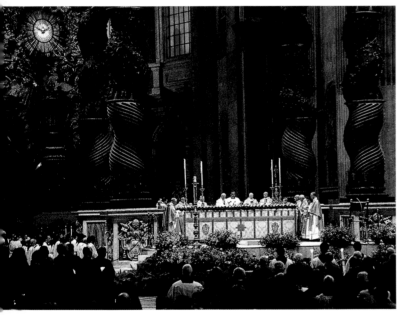

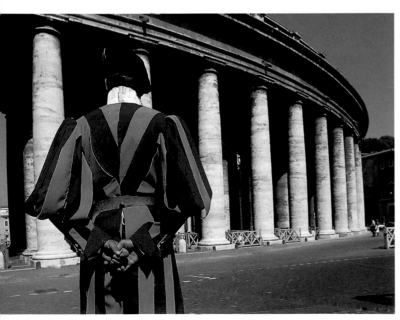

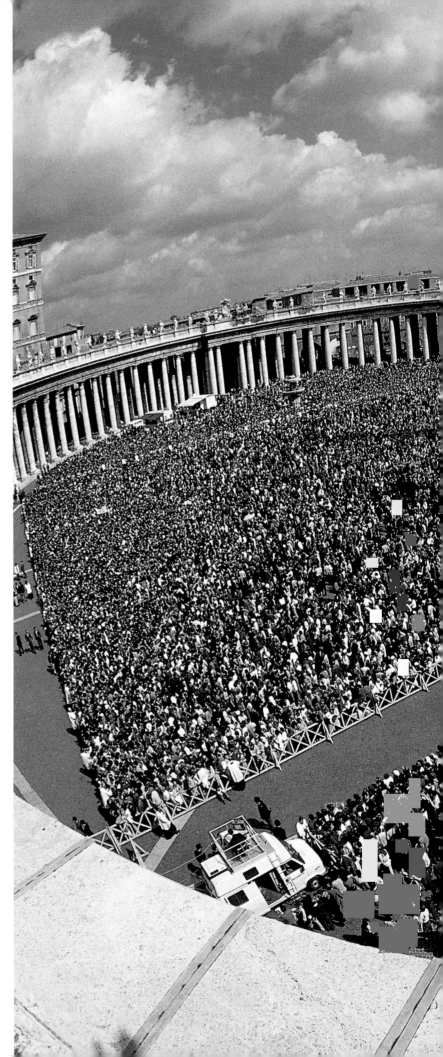

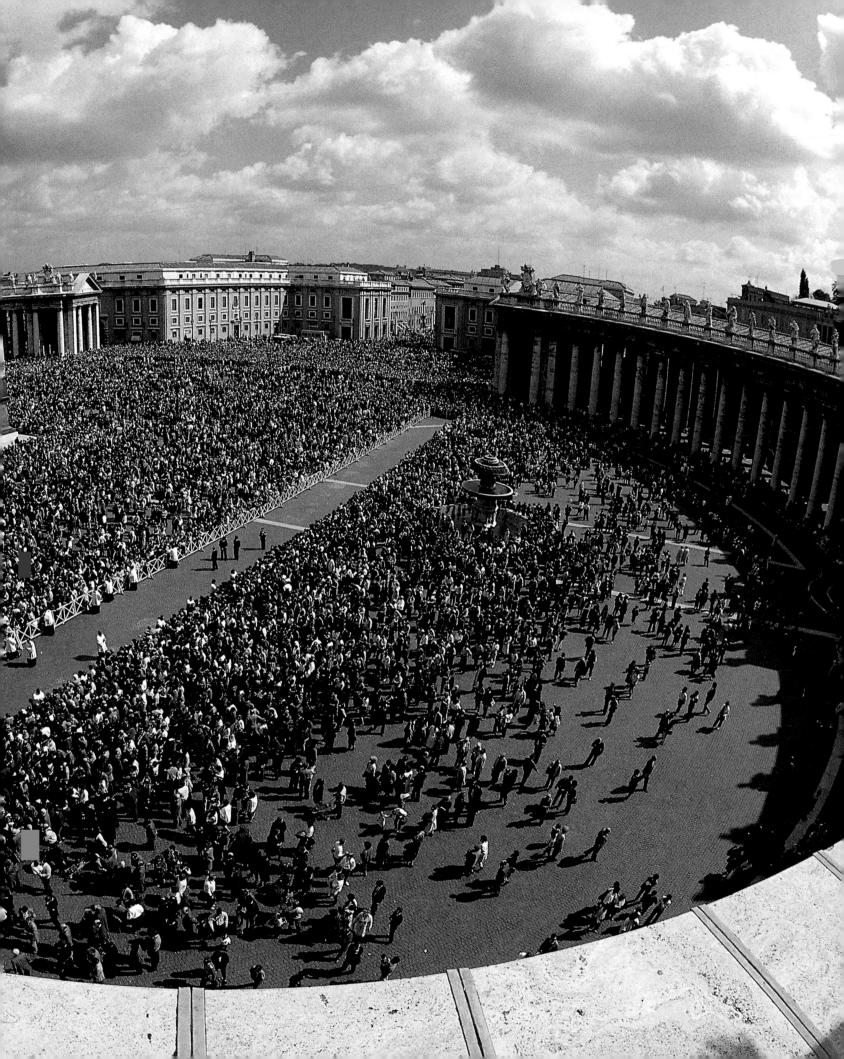

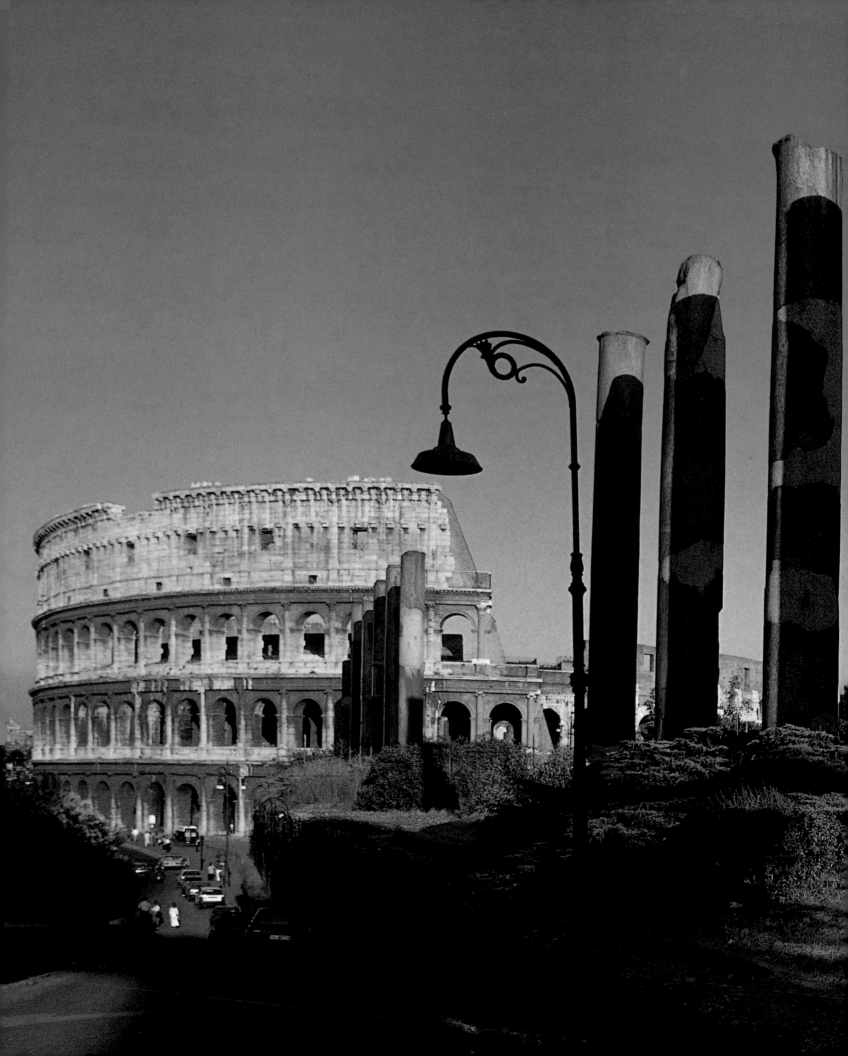

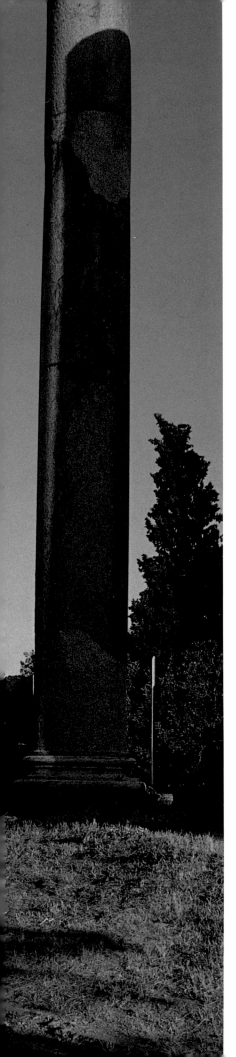

44-45 *Considered the very symbol of the eternity of Rome, the Colosseum was inaugurated by Titus in 80 A.D. after eight years of work. The huge amphitheater was destined for contests between gladiators and wild beasts.*

45 top left *The Roman Forum, a spectacular complex of temples, basilicas, and votive monuments, was the heart of public life in ancient Rome. From the 17th century on, the archeology of the site has gradually been revealed.*

45 bottom *The Arch of Constantine, one of the best preserved of all Roman arches, was built near the Colosseum to celebrate Constantine's victory over Maxentius.*

45 right *The large exedra of the Mercati Traiainei, dating from the first century A.D., consists of two stories of workshops surmounted by a splendid panoramic terrace.*

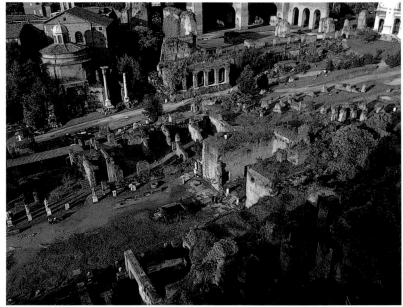

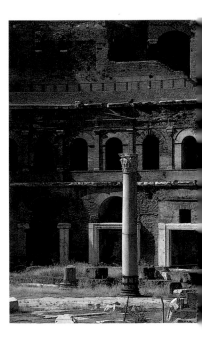

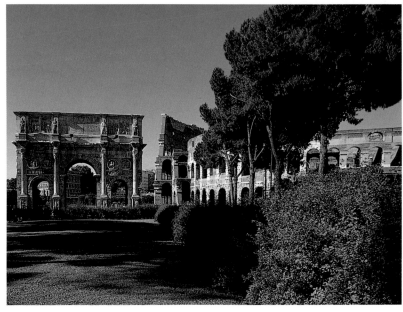

# Cosmopolitan Milan

Proud of its status as the principal commercial center in Italy, Milan has gained particular recognition in the field of international high fashion. The stock exchange here is the most important in the country, and its location is a sign of the leading position Milan holds in Italian industry. Busy, sometimes frenetic, Milan is among the most dynamic of northern European cities.

*46 left Even the clanging electric trams must fight their way through the many difficulties of Milanese traffic.*

*46 top right The 127-meter-high Pirelli skyscraper provides an excellent bird's-eye view over the city.*

*46 bottom right The Gallery is the site of some of the city's most elegant restaurants and is a traditional meeting place of the Milanese.*

*47 Built between 1865 and 1877, the Galleria Vittorio Emanuele II connects Piazza del Duomo and Piazza della Scala. Elegant metallic structures support the glass vaults which cast a luminous light on multicolored mosaics on the floor of the gallery.*

*48-49 After careful restoration, the Cathedral, with its 135 gothic spires, has regained its original splendor.*

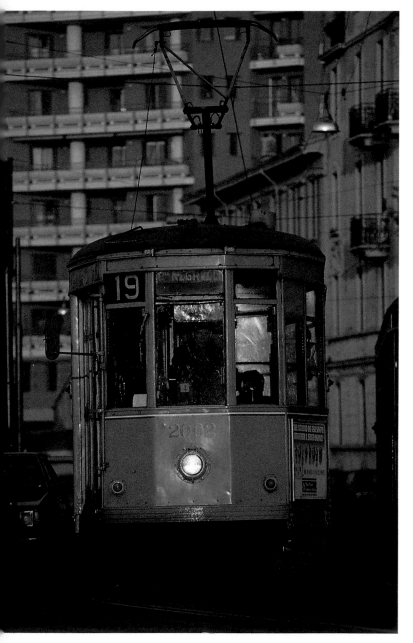

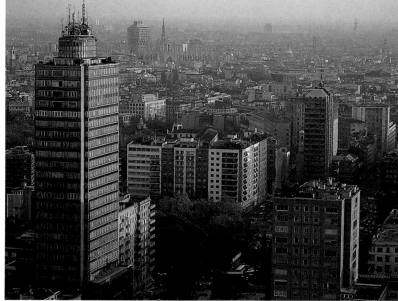

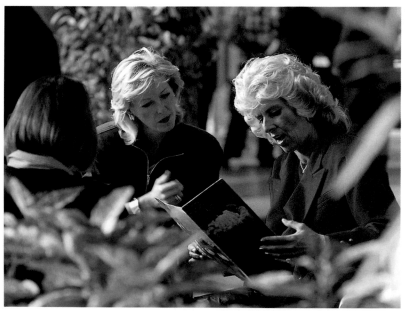

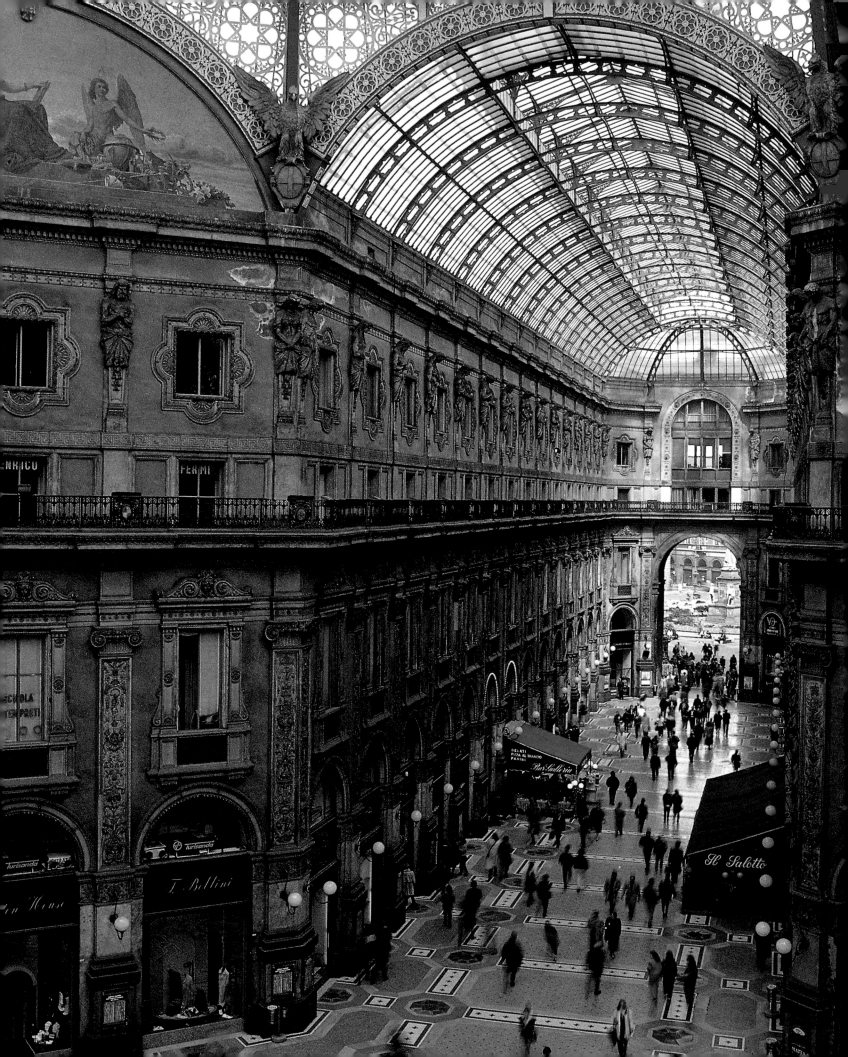

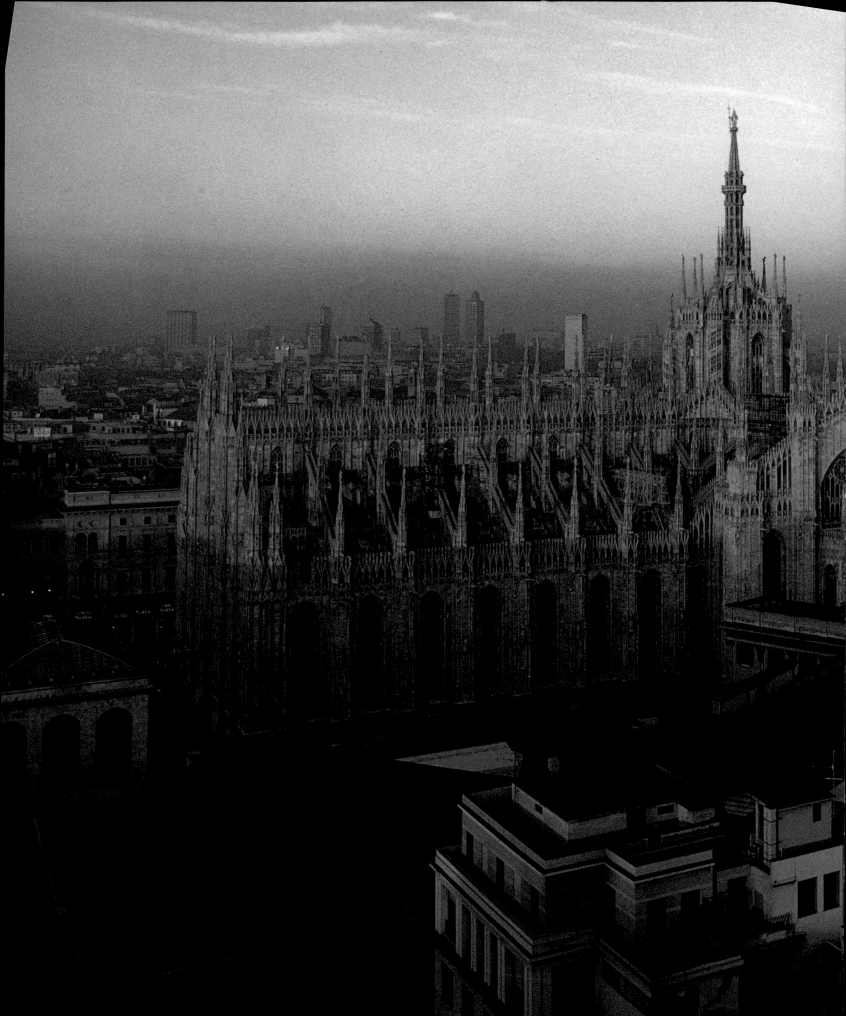

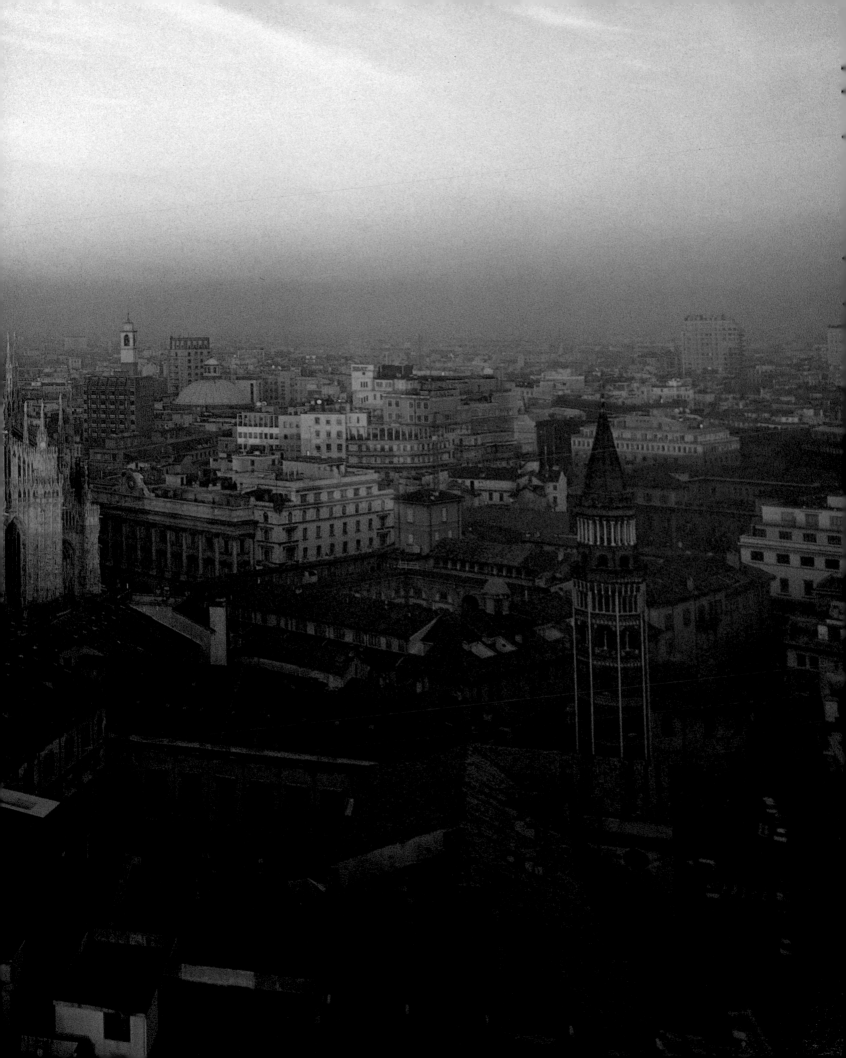

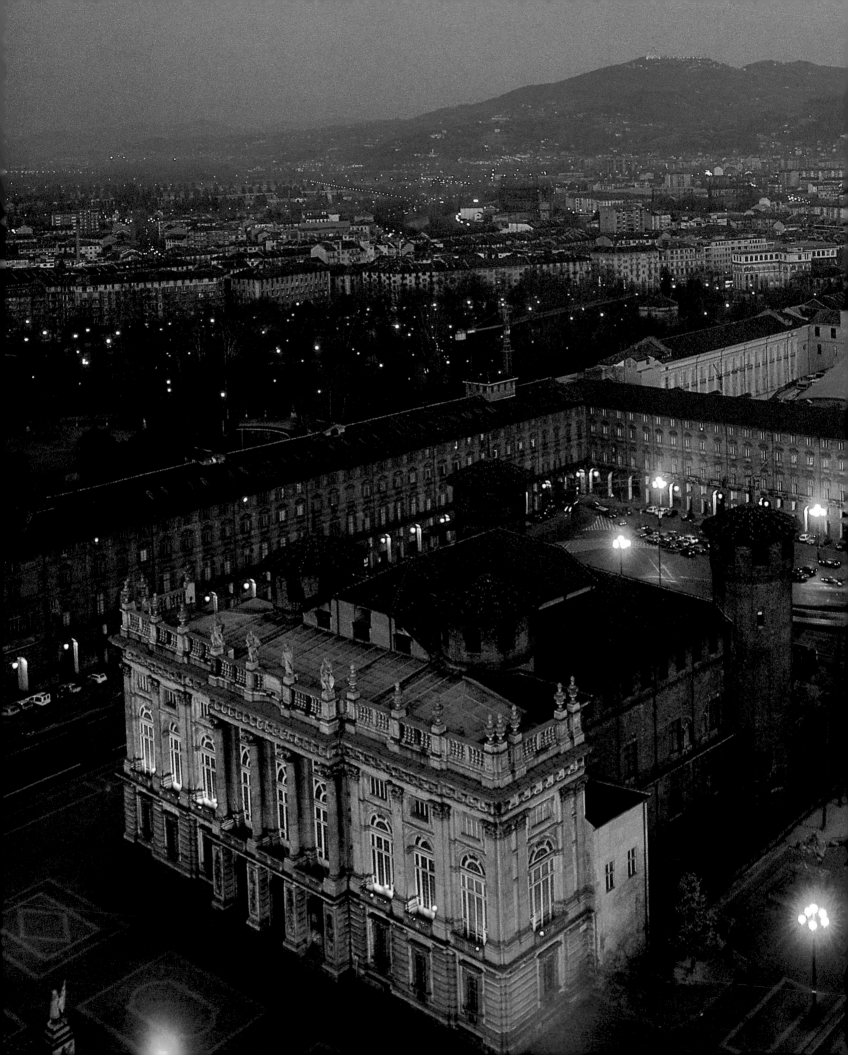

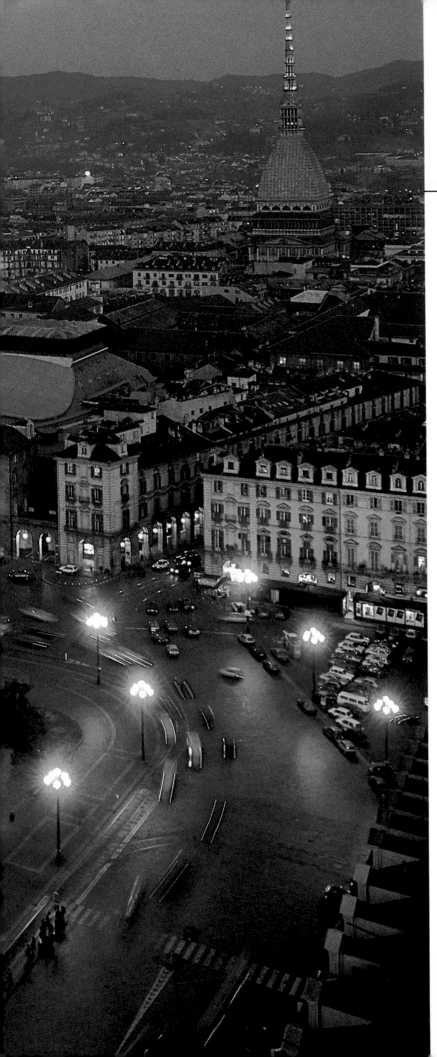

# Turin:
# the Lady

The visitor who arrives in Turin for the first time immediately realizes that he is in a setting very different from that of other Italian cities. This sensation is largely due to the dignified, refined, and slightly out-moded appearance of the layout of the city's streets and squares, a heritage dating from Roman times. Despite the industrial development

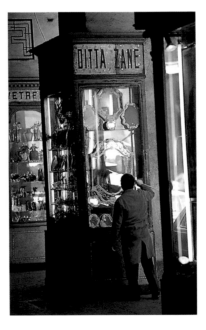

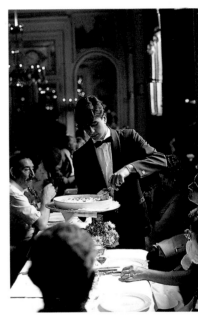

which has led to enormous expansion in the past three decades, the capital of the Piedmont region has remained true to its image as former capital of the Kingdom of Italy and prestigious cultural center. Its position on the banks of the Po, at the foot of the surrounding hills and in view of the Alps, further enhances the city's beauty.

50-51 *Palazzo Madama stands in the center of Piazza Castello. Its splendid Baroque facade, designed by Filippo Juvarra, was added in 1721.*

51 left *Turin's most traditional shops can be found under the porticoes that line Via Po.*

51 right *In the elegant restaurants of old Turin, the culinary tradition of the Piedmont is kept alive.*

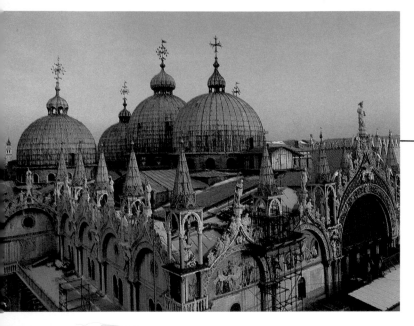

# Venice, Labyrinth of Water

Together with Florence and Rome, Venice, the ancient Queen of the Adriatic, holds a place as one of the major centers of Italian art. The city's magnificent palaces reveal the influence of Oriental, Italian Baroque, and Renaissance styles. Since Venice is built on an archipelago of more than 100 small islands, the principal thoroughfares of the city consist of innumerable canals which are usually crowded with boats of all sorts. Of these, the slender gondola is the most unique.

To discover the most hidden corners of the city, walk down the narrow, winding lanes which suddenly open out onto "campielli," the settings for the most authentic Venetian life.

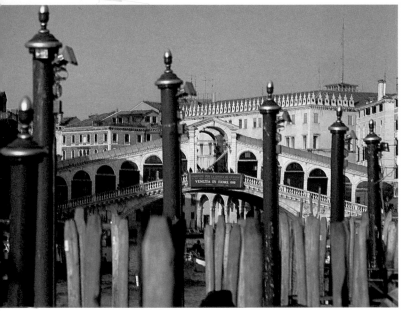

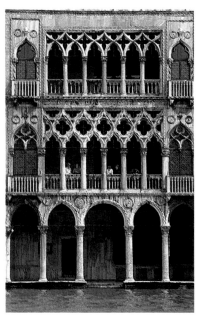

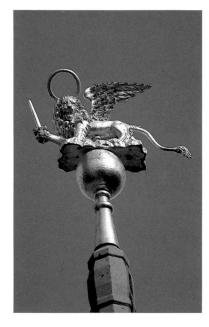

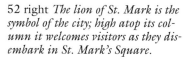

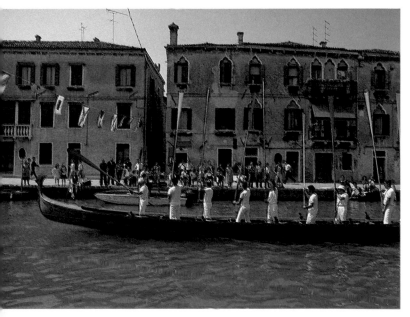

52 top left *When the soft, golden light of the setting sun envelops its cupolas, St. Mark's Basilica is a magical place.*

52 center left *The Rialto Bridge, the largest and best-known bridge in Venice, was built in 1592. It is in the heart of one of the city's best shopping areas.*

52 bottom left *Each year, the Vogalonga, along with the Regata Storica and the Festa del Redentore, commemorate the maritime traditions of the old Venetian Republic.*

52 center *The Ca' d'Oro (the Golden House) on the Grand Canal is a masterpiece of Venetian gothic architecture. Its name comes from the fact that it was once covered in gold.*

52 right *The lion of St. Mark is the symbol of the city; high atop its column it welcomes visitors as they disembark in St. Mark's Square.*

53 *The multicolored marble facade and the skillful design of walls and supporting arches give an impression of extreme lightness to the Doge's Palace.*

54-55 *Two Venetians in costume strike a pose with the island of San Giorgio in the background.*

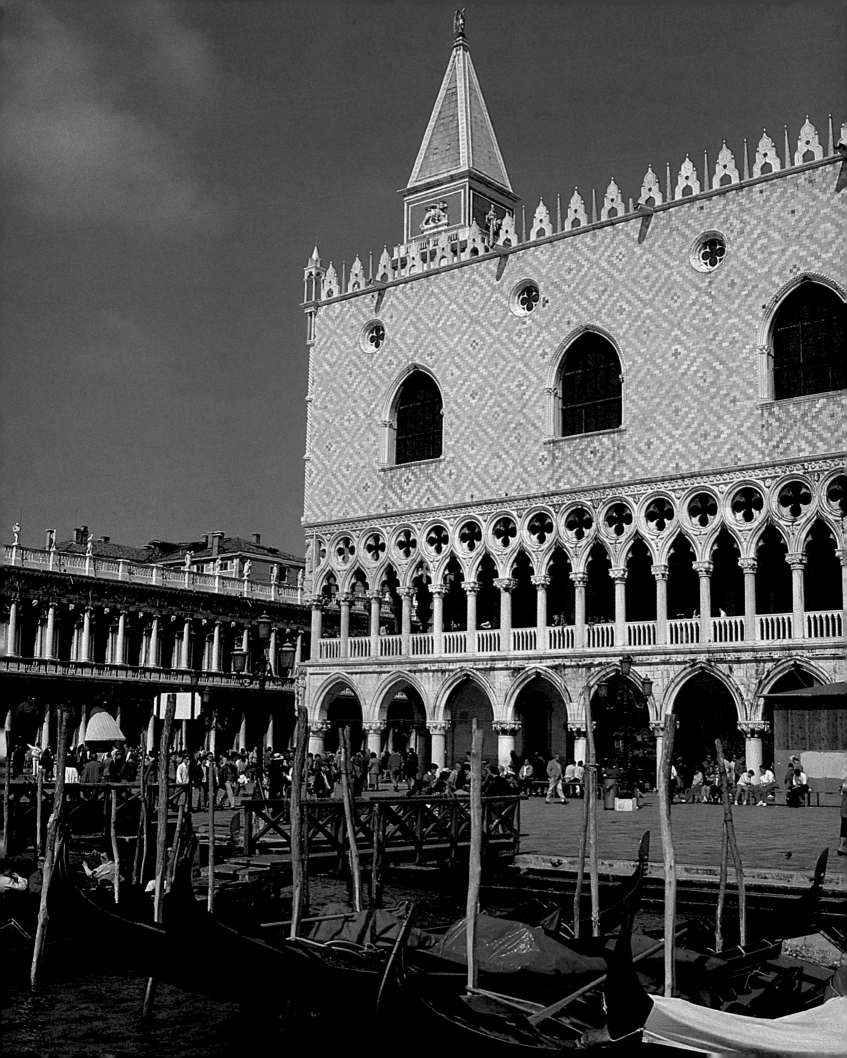

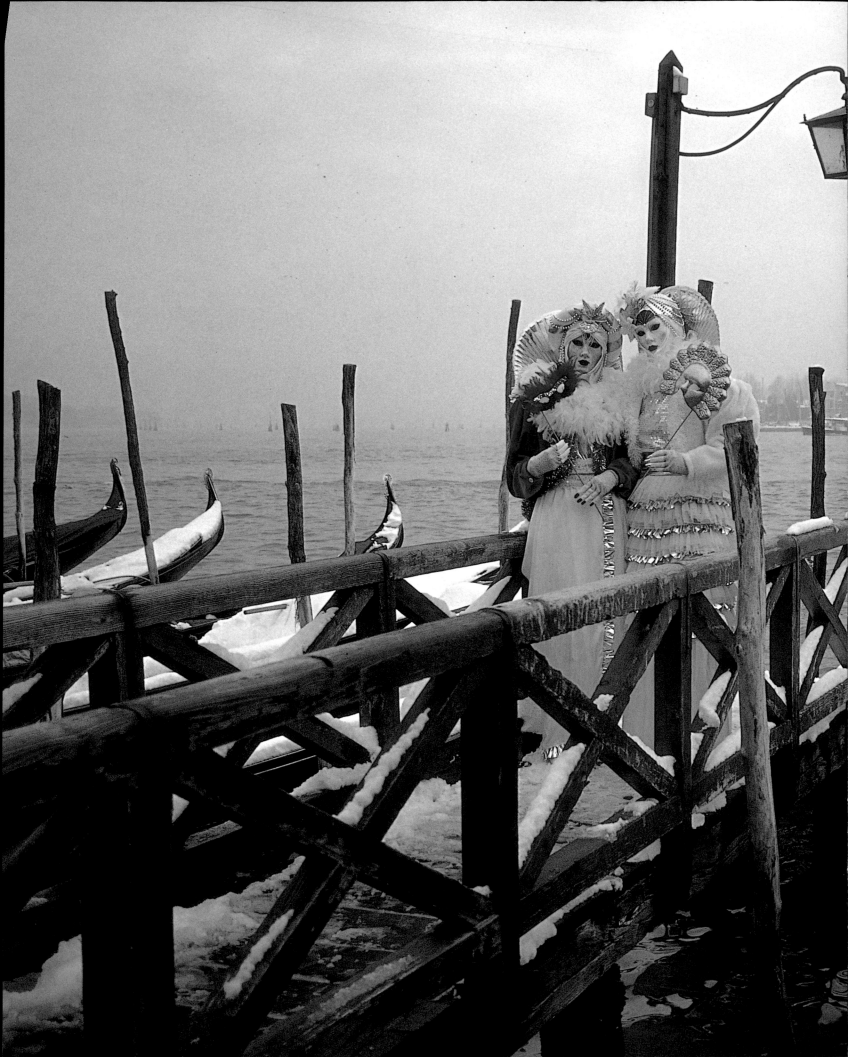

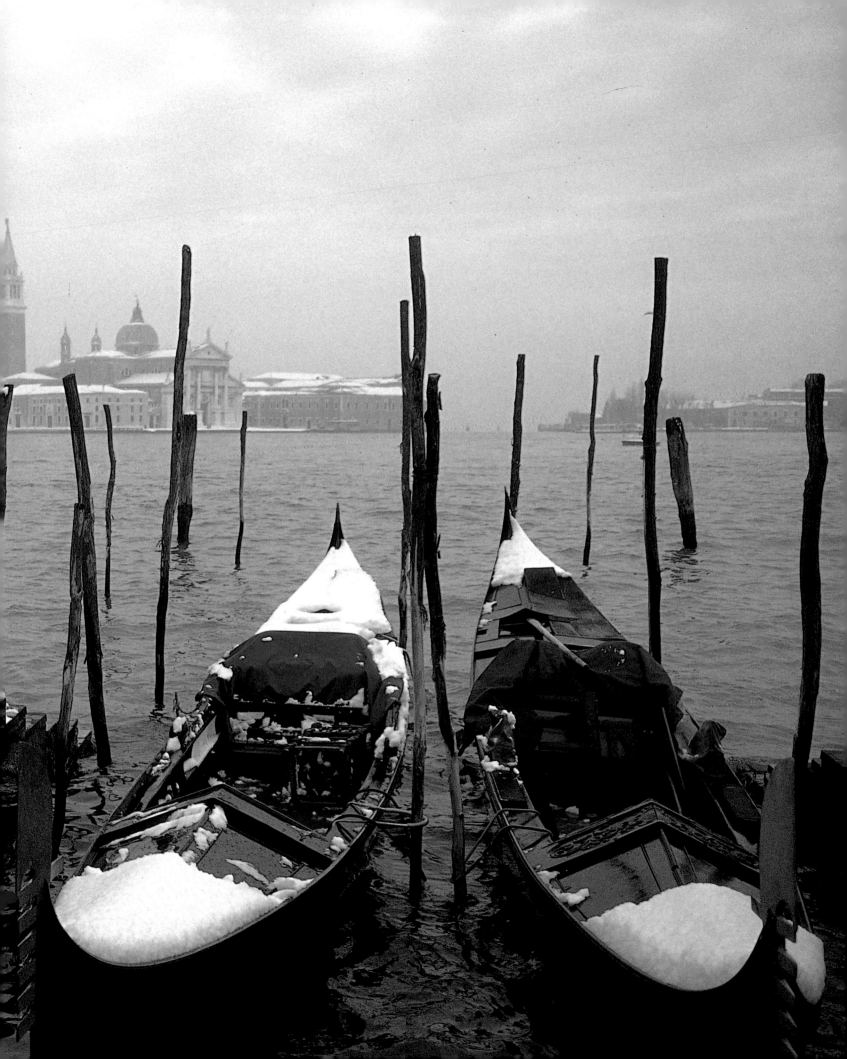

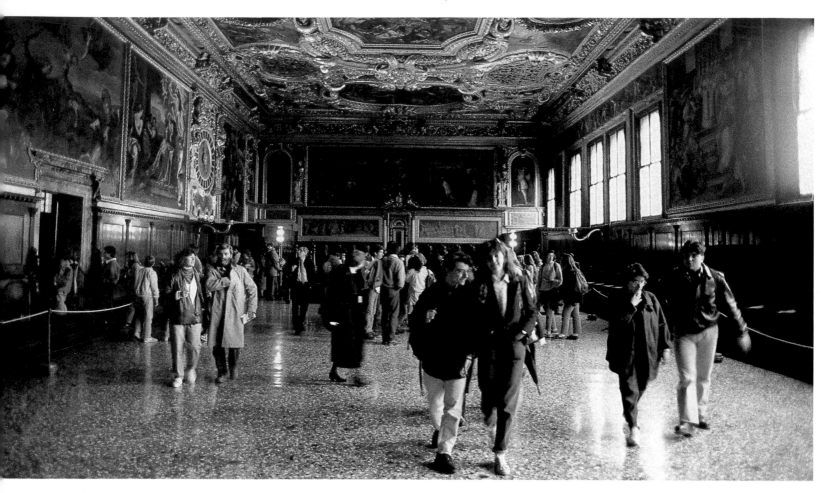

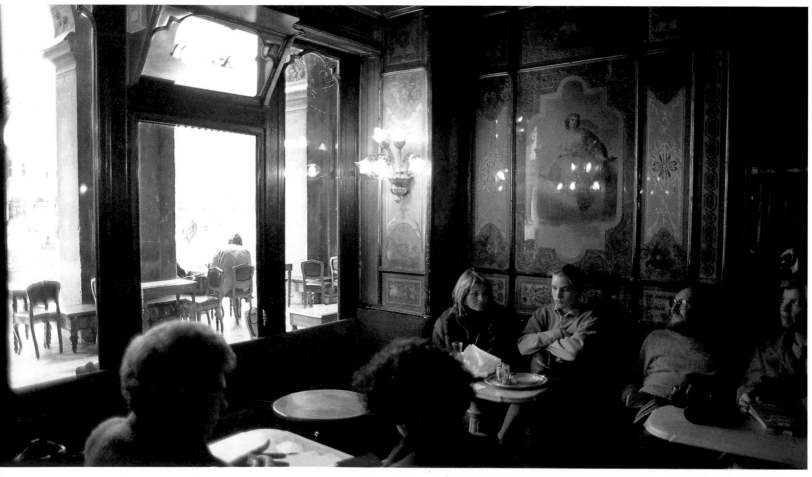

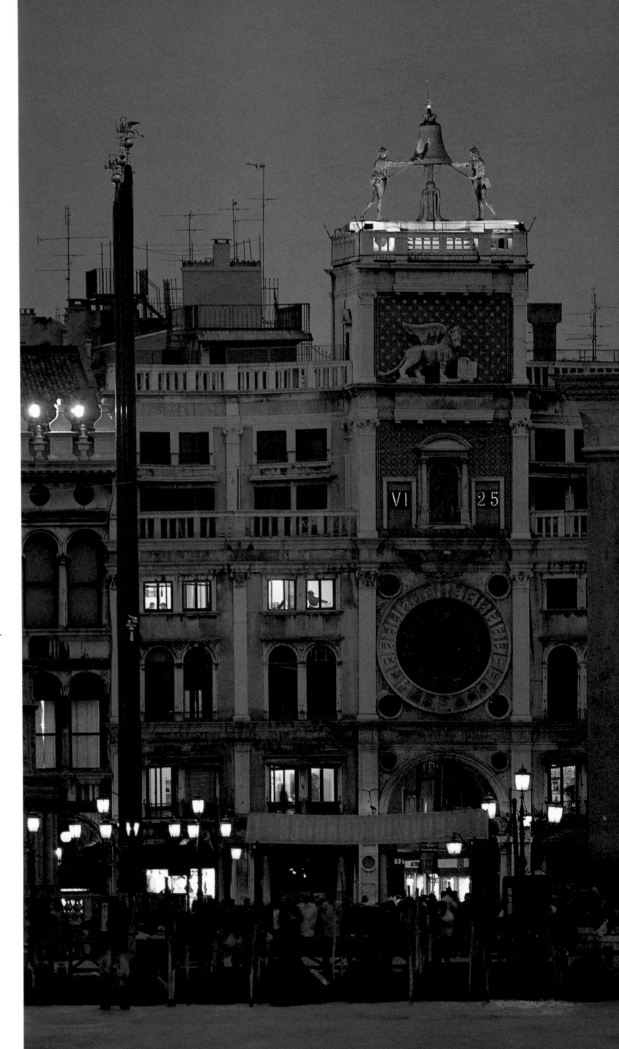

56 top *The richly decorated rooms inside the Doge's Palace feature carved ceilings adorned with friezes and painted panels.*

56 bottom *Now famous for its chic atmosphere, the Caffè Florian was once the setting for patriotic conspiracies during the Austrian occupation.*

57 *At the top of the clock tower in St. Mark's Square, the famous animated statues of two Moors have been striking the hours every day since 1497.*

# Magnificent Florence

On the border of the upper and lower Arno Valley, enclosed by a circle of hills covered with olive trees, pines, and cypresses, is Florence, the cradle of the Italian language and the city where Dante began writing. The history of Florence is closely connected with that of the Medici family, the benefactors of some of the most illustrious Renaissance artists. Leonardo, Michelangelo, and Botti-celli made Florence the stronghold of ideal beauty. Lorenzo de' Medici, known as the Magnificent, was himself a talented poet as well as a generous patron of the arts. It is no wonder, given such an illustrious background, that Florence has made a great contribution to Italian civilization and is still an important cultural center with a unique and unmistakable historical character.

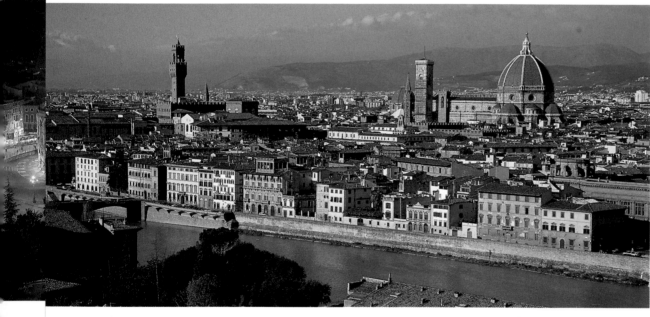

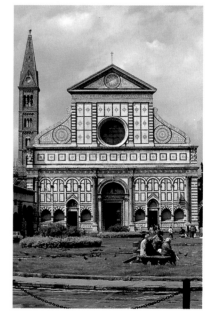

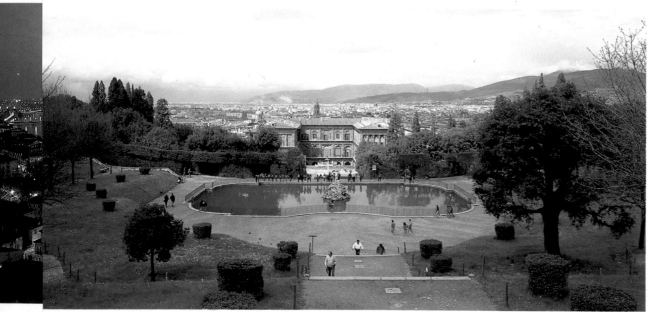

60 top left *From Piazzale Miche-langelo a panoramic view of the city is divided in two by the Arno River.*

60 bottom left *The Boboli Garden on the grounds of Palazzo Pitti displays the dramatic landscaping typical of gardens designed in Italy in the second half of the 16th century.*

60 right *The Church of Santa Maria Novella is a hybrid of two styles. The lower half was completed in the gothic period, and the upper half was designed by Leon Battista Alberti 100 years later.*

61 *Giotto's bell tower and Brunelleschi's immense Cathedral dome tower over the red roofs of the city.*

62-63 *Ponte Vecchio is lined by two rows of goldsmith's and jeweler's shops.*

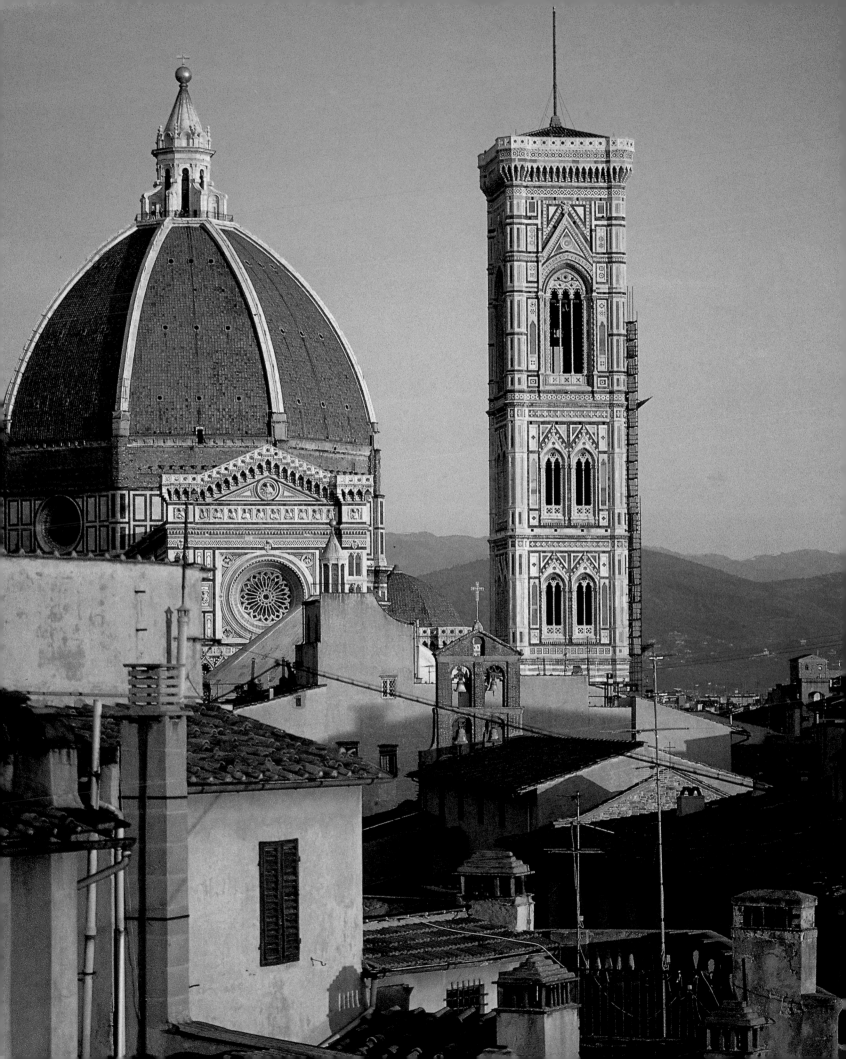

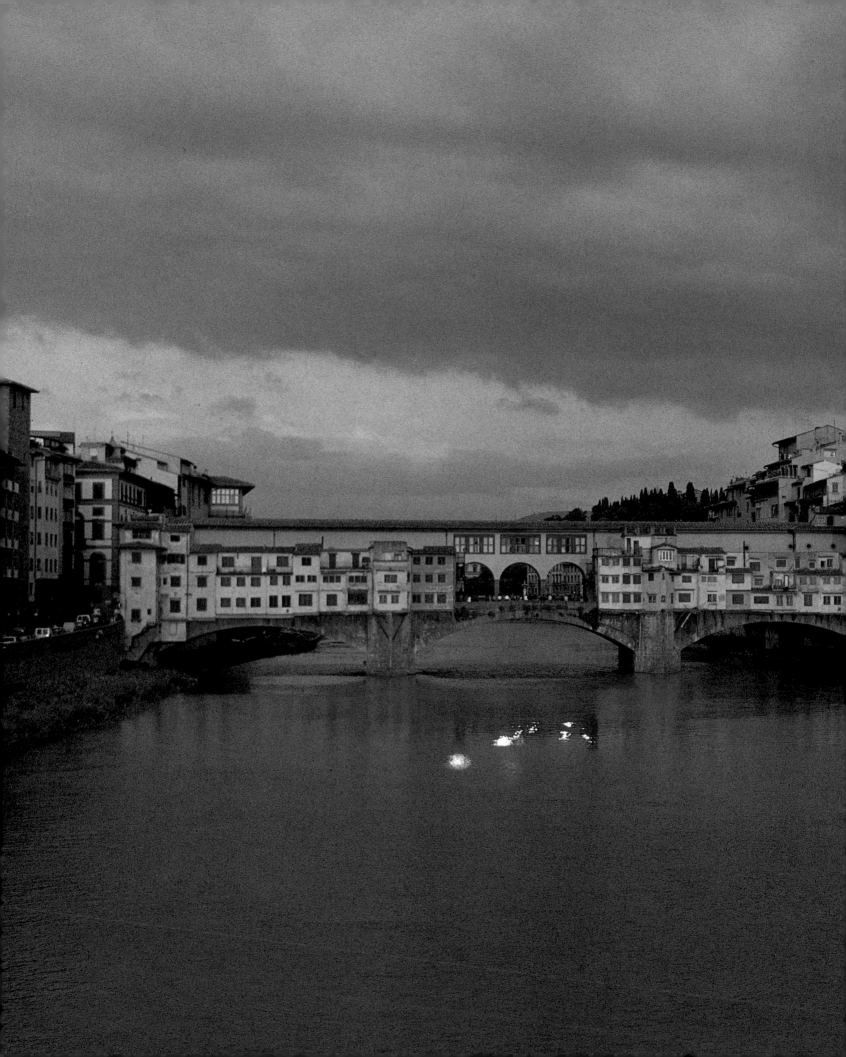

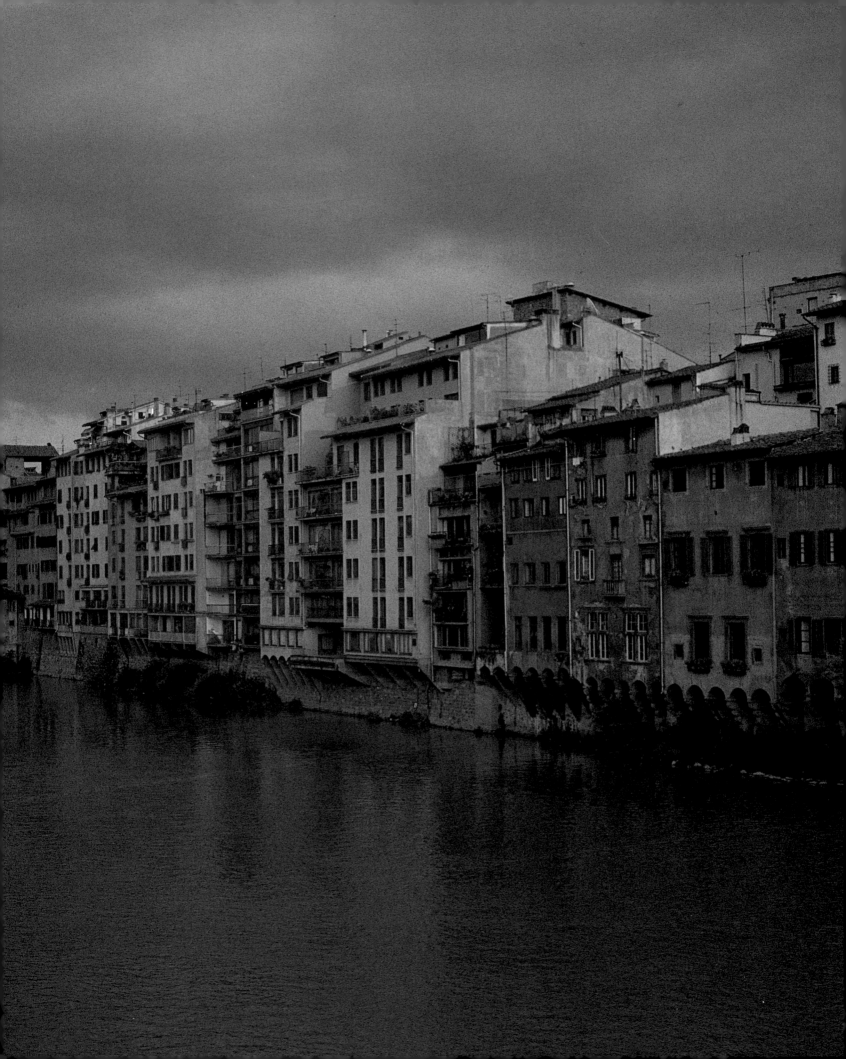

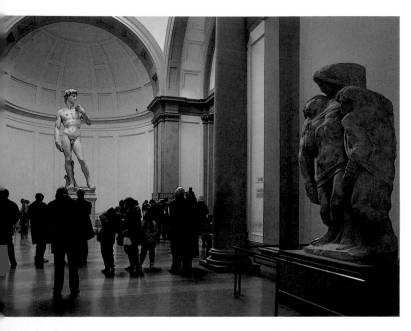

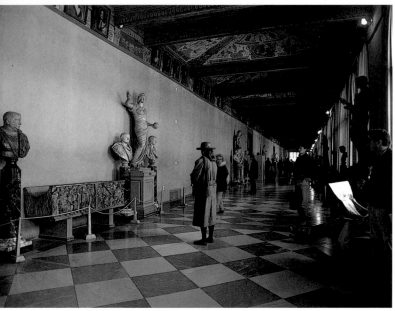

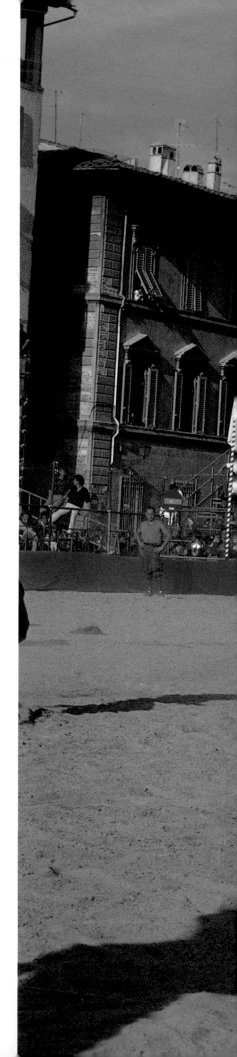

64 top *The Galleria dell'Accademia is famous for its sculptures by Michelangelo: the Palestrina Pietà, Saint Matthew, the four incomplete Slaves originally designed for the tomb of Pope Julius II in Rome, and the famous David, a copy of which can be seen in Piazza della Signoria.*

64 center and bottom *Masterpieces of Italian painting from all periods are housed in the Uffizi, the single most important gallery for Italian art in the world. Valuable works from other European countries can be seen here, as well.*

64-65 *On the first Sunday in May and on June 24, football matches are held in Piazza Santa Croce. The events, which date back to the 16th century, are spectacular and rather violent.*

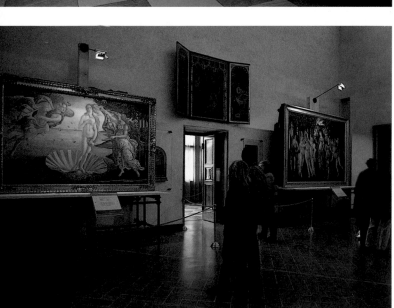

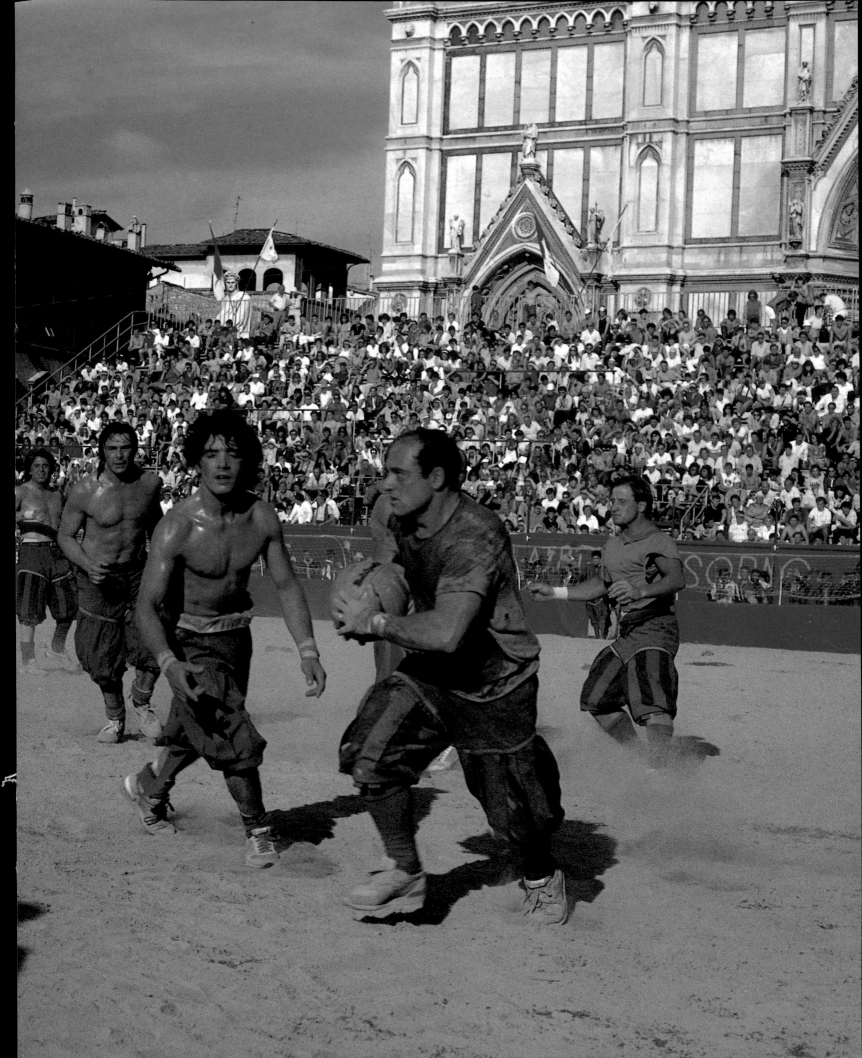

# Siena, Reflection of a Another Age

Each year on July 2nd and August 16th, a famous horse race called the Palio takes place in Siena's Piazza del Campo. The race is preceded by a procession in costume in which all the "contrade," or city quarters, take part. The origin of this tradition dates back to the 14th century when, on the second day of July, a Medici soldier shot at an effigy of the Madonna. To make up for this sacrilege, a church was built and the Palio was organized.

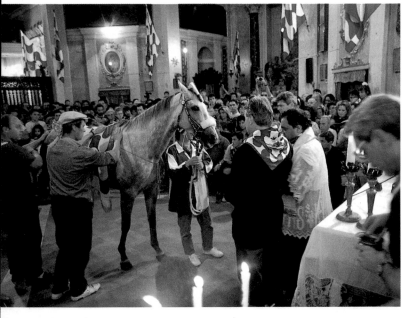

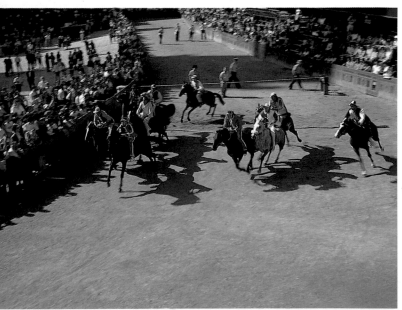

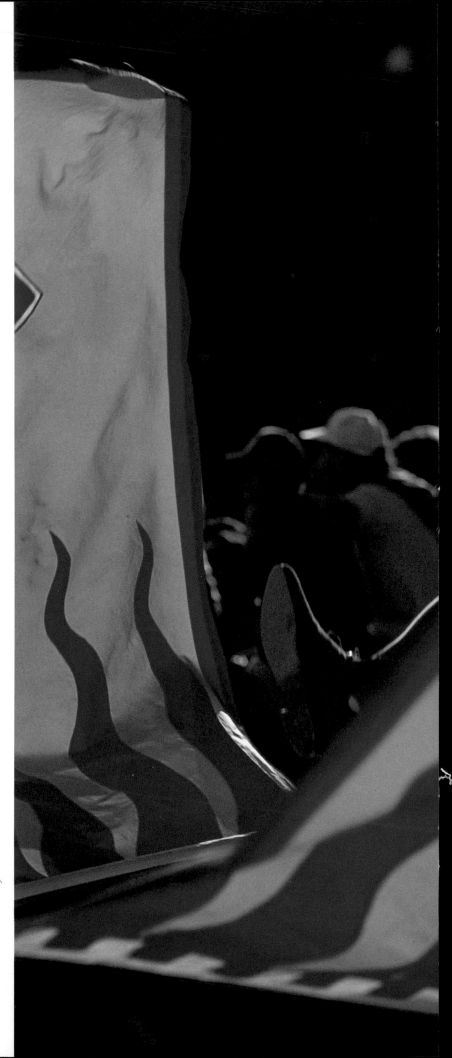

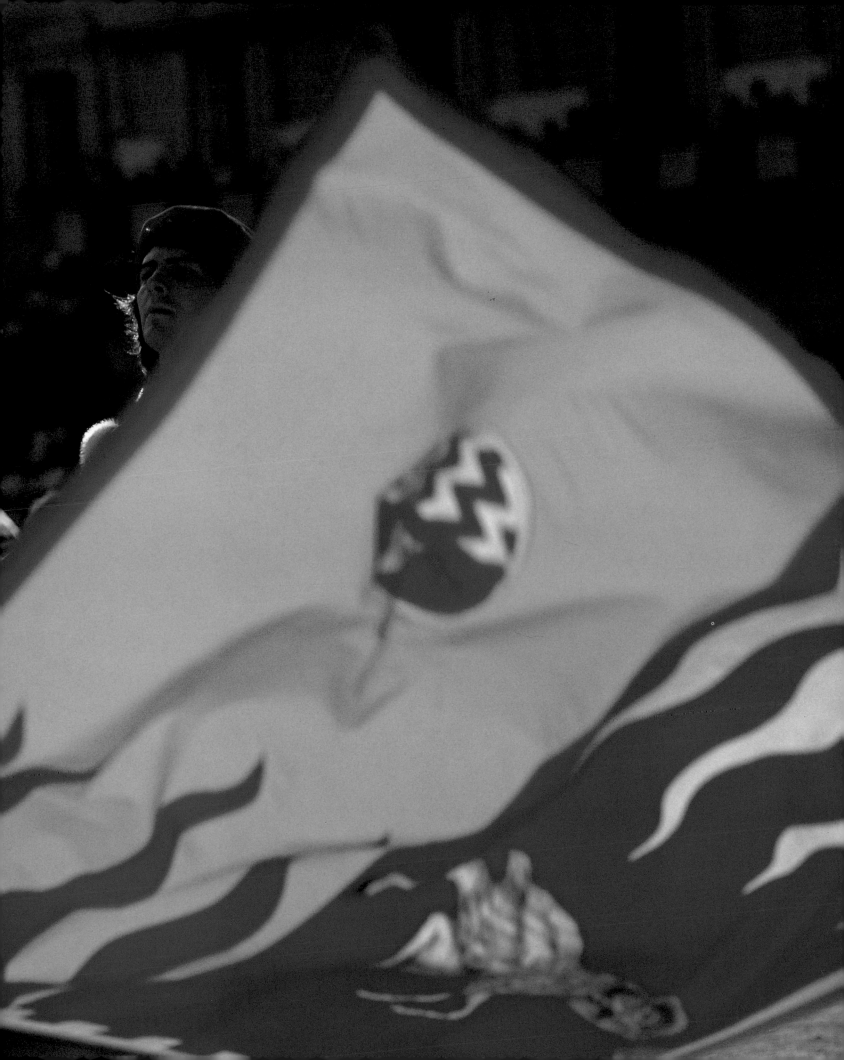

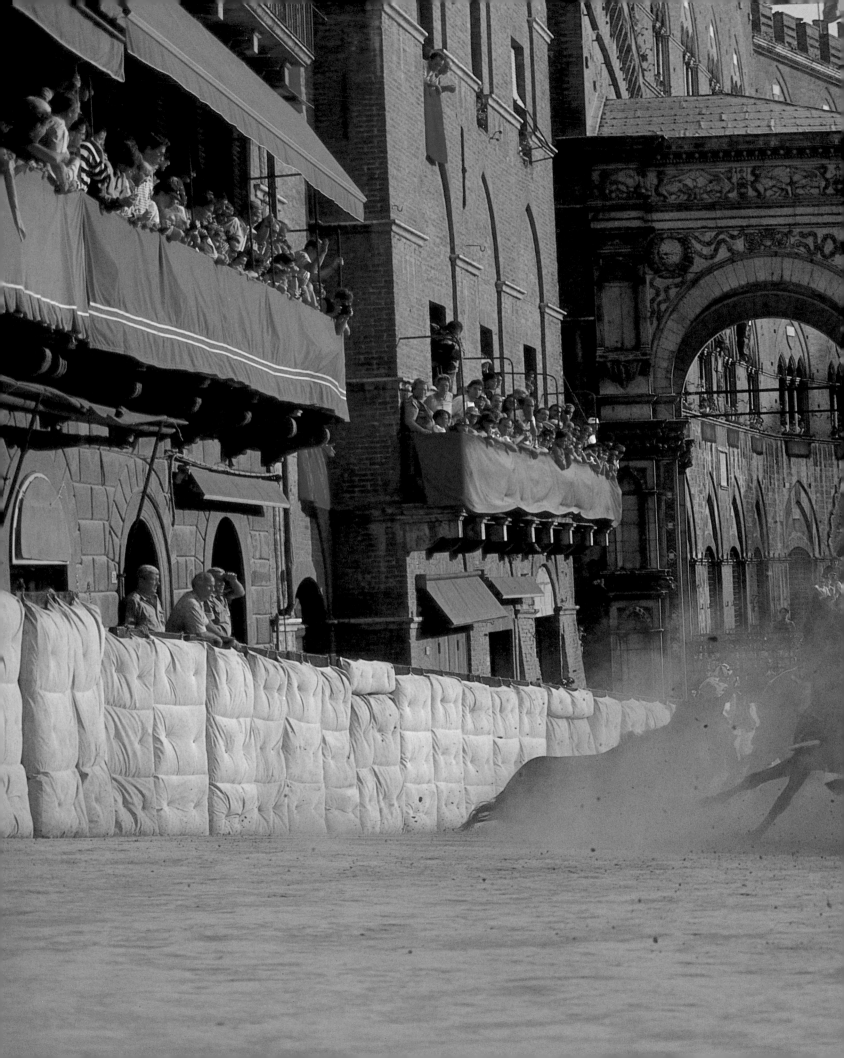

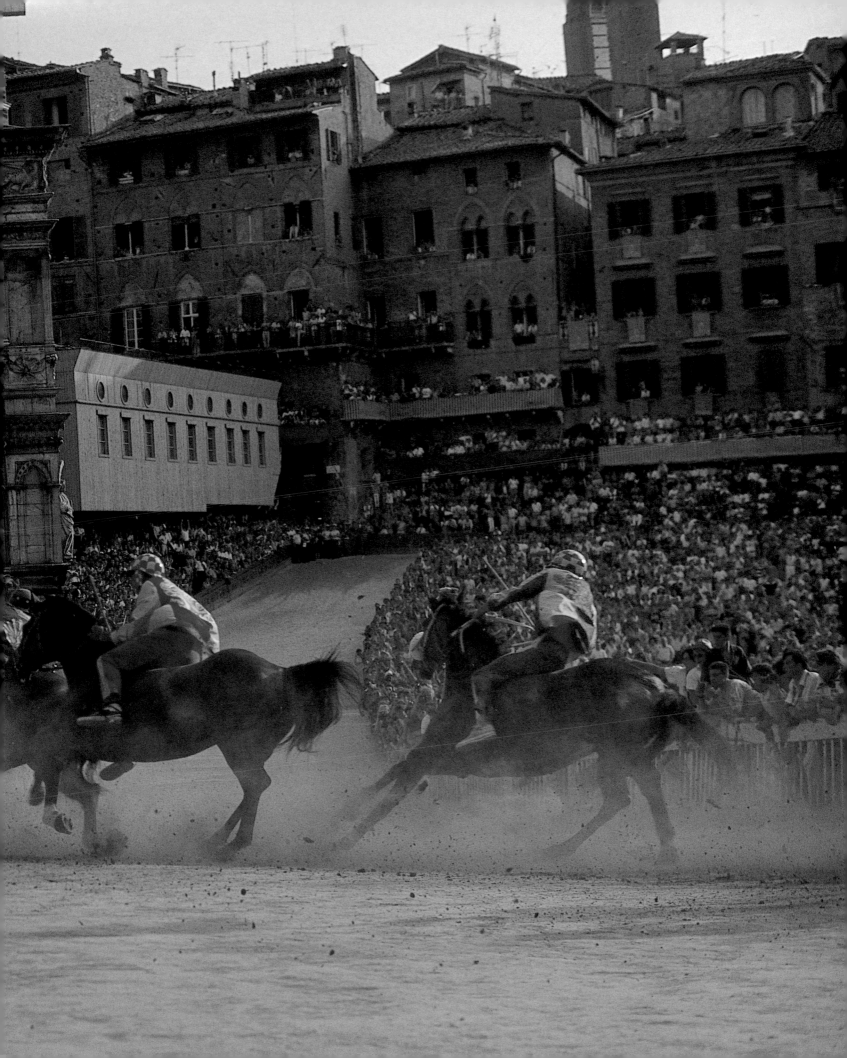

# Naples,
# the Taste of Surprise

"See Naples and die" is a well-known saying, and in fact it would be difficult to find another city with an equally enchanting geography and atmosphere. Overlooking a wide gulf, its houses built on the surrounding hills with Vesuvius on guard in the background, Naples provides one of the most spectacular panoramas in the Mediterranean. While the misery and heroism of Naples has been so well captured in the films of De Sica and Totò, the true soul of the city is to be found in the popular quarters that surround the center of the old part of the city. Here, behind the crumbling facades and closed doors in front of which the boys play football, are incredibly beautiful courtyards and staircases.

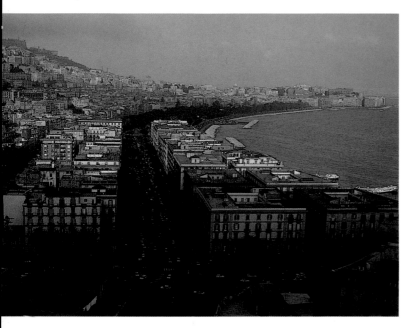

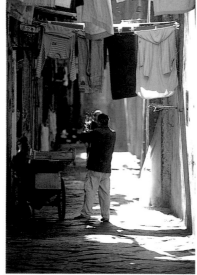

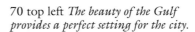

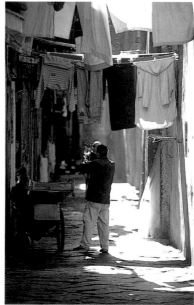

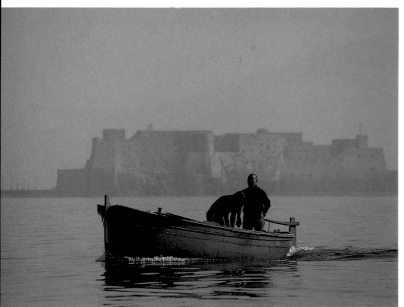

70 top left *The beauty of the Gulf provides a perfect setting for the city.*

70 bottom left *These fishermen casting their nets into the waters of the Gulf perpetuate the maritime traditions of the city.*

70 right *The lines of wash hanging out to dry add touches of color to the lanes in the popular quarters of Naples.*

70-71 *The picturesque cove of Mergellina at the foot of Posillipo Hill is one of the most poetic and celebrated spots in Naples.*

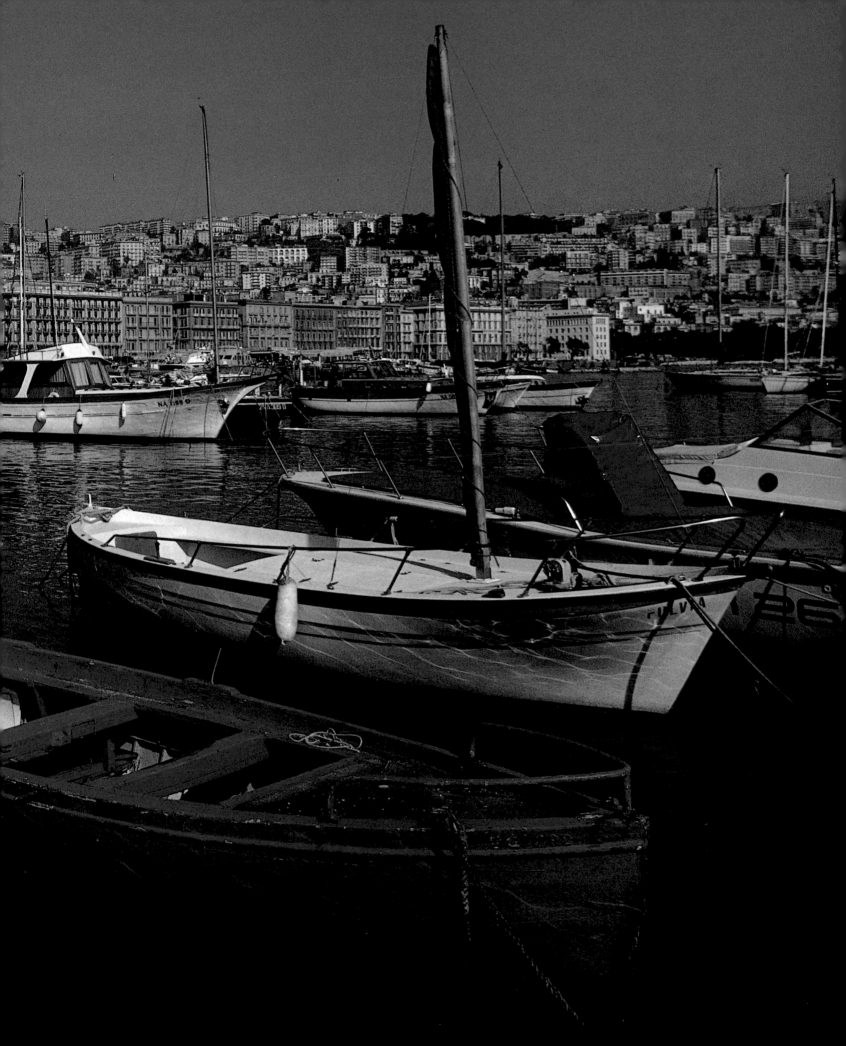

# Pompei and Paestum, Traces of the Past

Founded at the foot of Vesuvius by the Oscans during Roman times, Pompei was a flourishing city when Vesuvius erupted during the night of August 24th in 79 A.D. The town was literally covered with a shower of red-hot lava. Preserved by the volcanic stone, the city now provides us with a complete example of the layout of towns during the Roman Empire. The city of Paestum had a different destiny. It was founded in the 7th Century B.C. by Greek colonists and given the name of Posidonia before being buried by time and forgotten by man. Until the 18th century, when a number of adventurous foreign travelers were attracted by the romanticism of the ruins, Paestum remained hidden and ignored amid the marshes and forests that held its treasures almost intact.

*72 left The "peristilium," a charac-teristic of Greek houses, was an open area embellished with columns and often a central garden.*

*72 right The walls of the houses of Pompei were decorated with tempera paintings.*

*73 As Pompei gradually became a flourishing commercial center, its houses were modified and turned into elegant dwellings.*

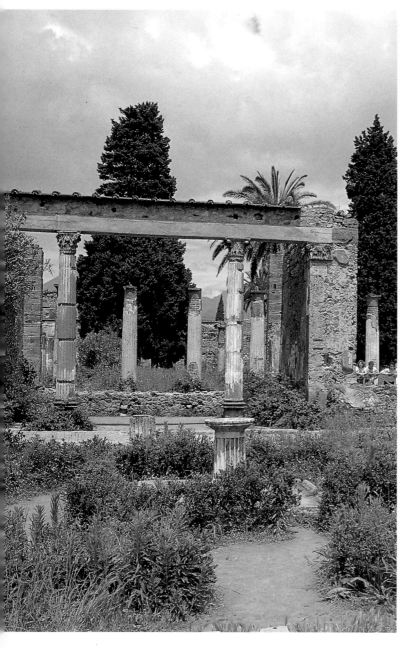

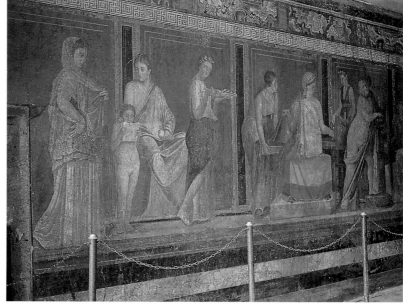

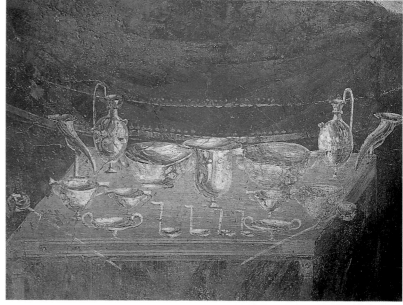

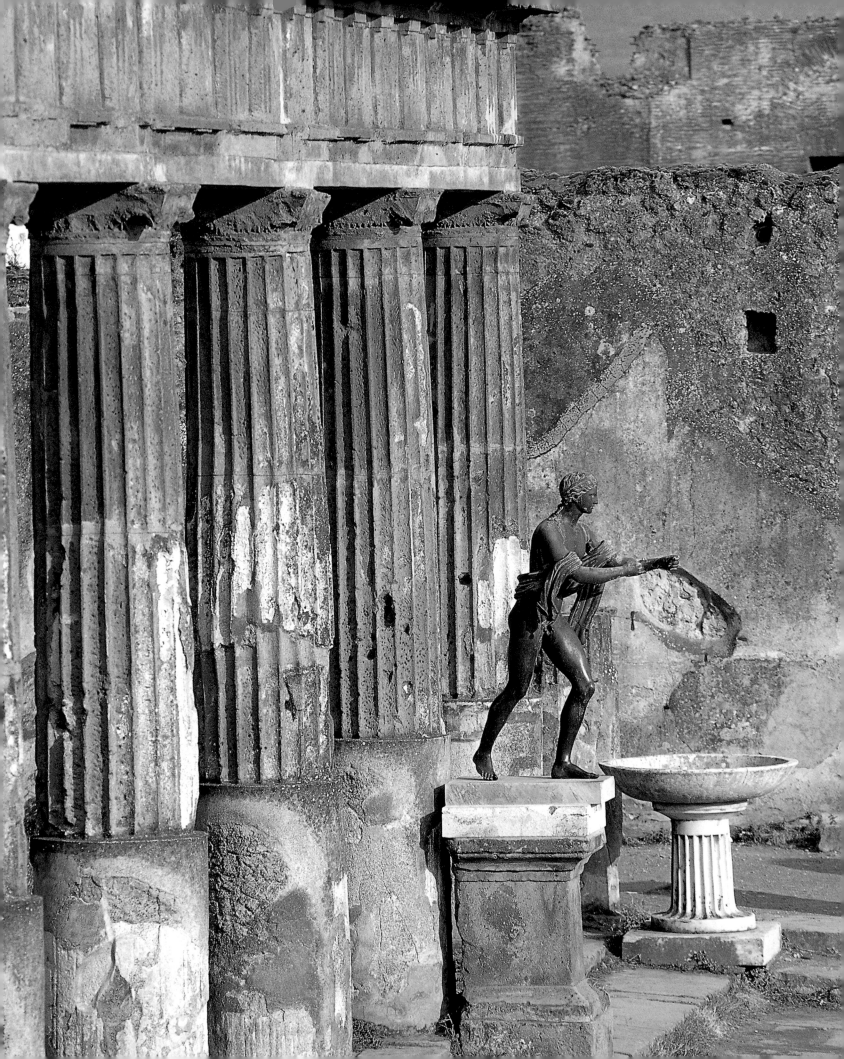

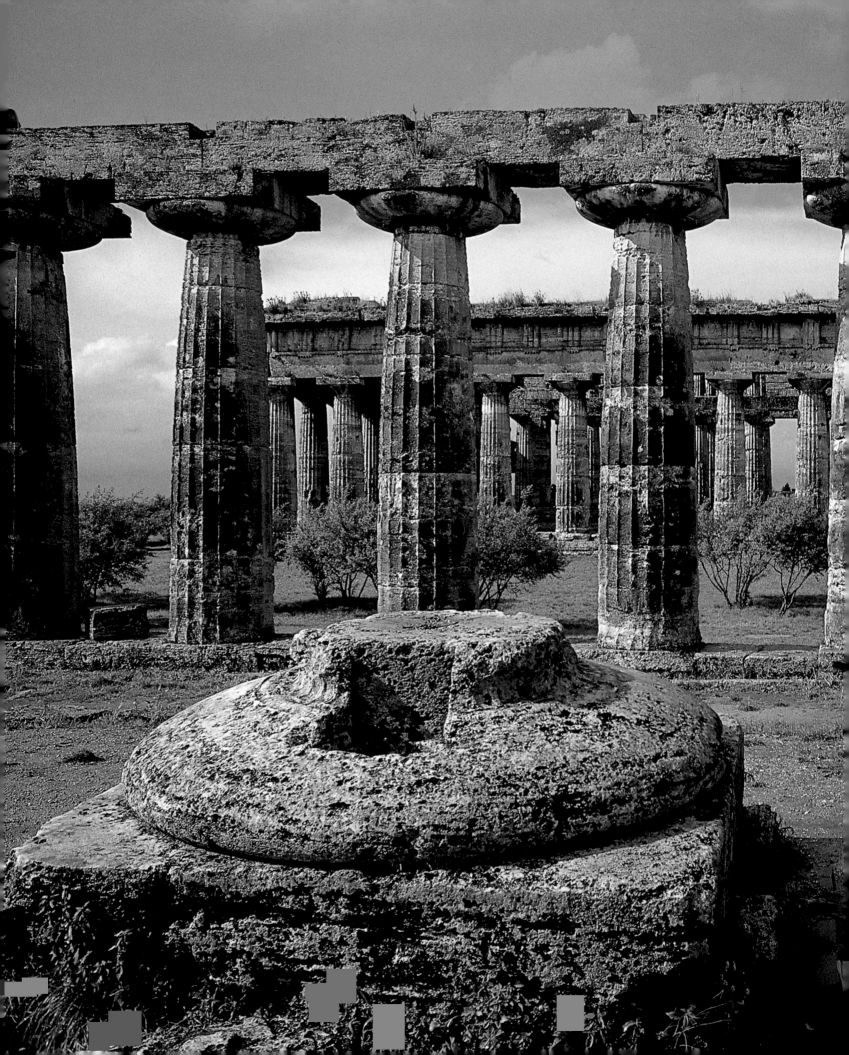

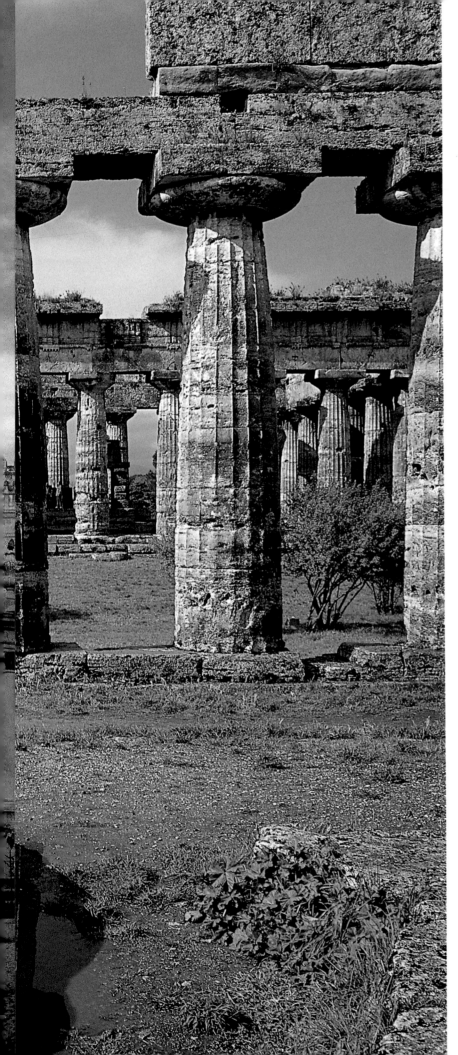

75 top *The temple of Neptune is one of the most beautiful and best-preserved Doric temples remaining at Paestum.*

75 bottom *The temple of Ceres was dedicated to the god Athena and later converted to a church in the Middle Ages.*

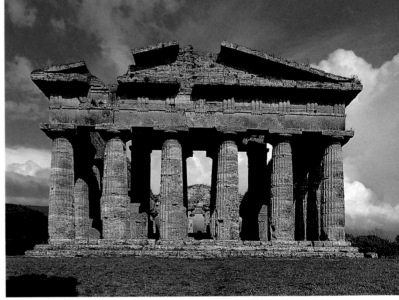

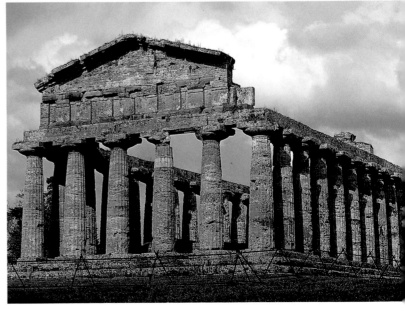

# Agrigento, Selinunte, Segesta: Where Nature and History Complement One Another

A journey through the oldest remains of ancient Sicily has always been a return to the natural elements. Builders in the classical world knew the intimate secrets of the island and how to use most effectively the subtle play of light and color in the landscape to their advantage. The mystical bond which united the Greek colonies to the Divine presence was so strongly felt that each city boasted the protection of a God or a supernatural hero. Even today it can still be felt by the more attentive visitor who can sense the mystery of proportion among the ancient stones. The theaters and temples of Selinunte, Agrigento, and Segesta represent a balance between architecture and the natural landscape which has yet to be equaled.

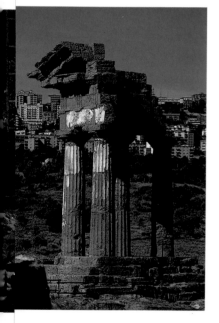

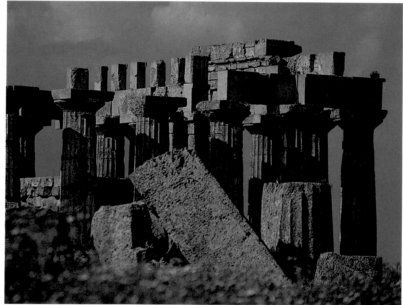

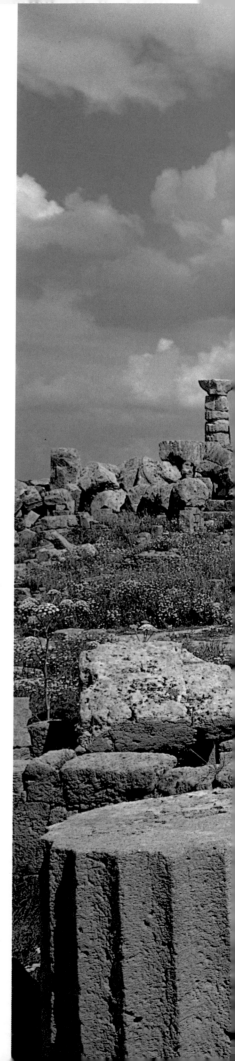

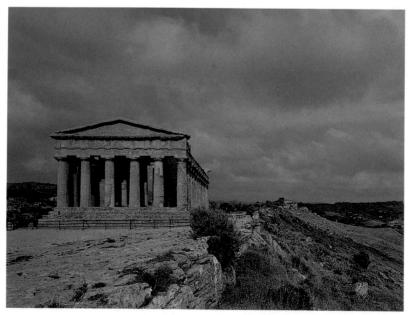

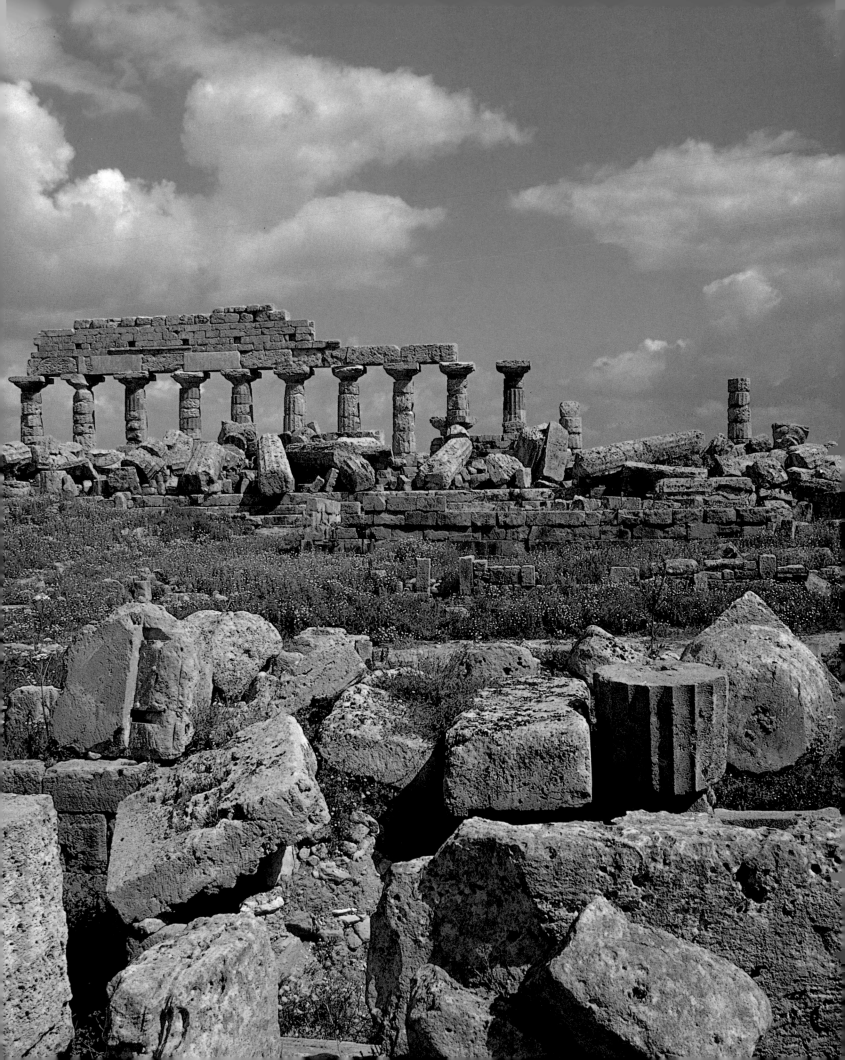

78 top left *A group of four columns is all that remains of the temple of Castor and Pollux.*

78 top right and 78-79 *The largest temple at Selinunte is Temple C, with 17 columns along the sides and 6 columns along the front.*

78 bottom right *In the valley of the Temples at Agrigento, a number of sacred buildings date from the Greek epoch. Of these, the best preserved is the Concordia Temple.*

80 left *Segesta was founded in the 12th century B.C.; its Doric temple and Greek amphitheater remain as monuments to that epoch.*

80-81 *The temple of Agrigento, dedicated to Hercules, dates from 520 A.D. Formed by a perimeter of 38 columns, it is one of the largest and most spectacular of its kind.*

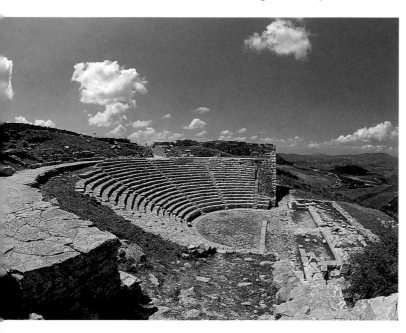

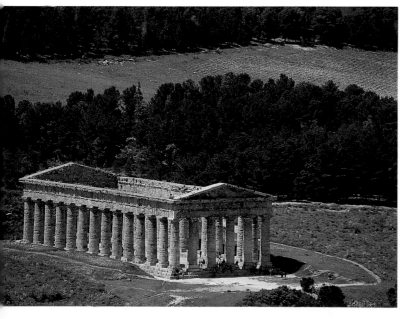

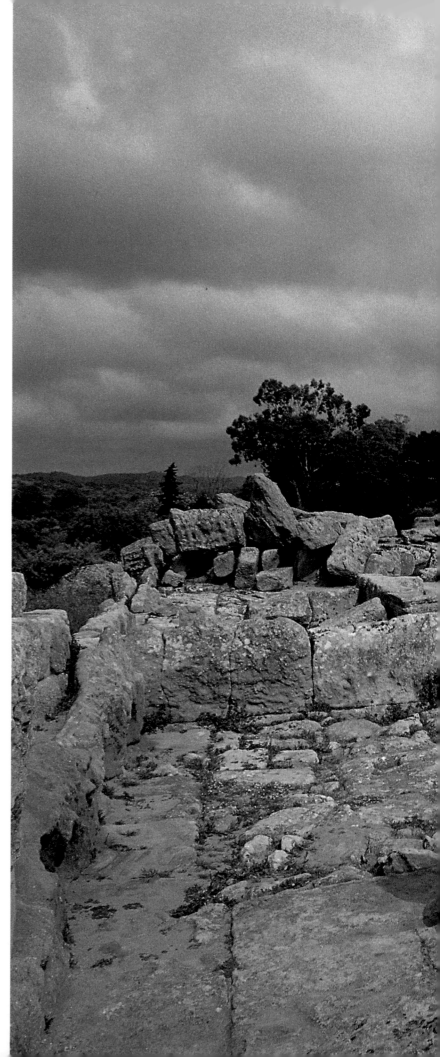

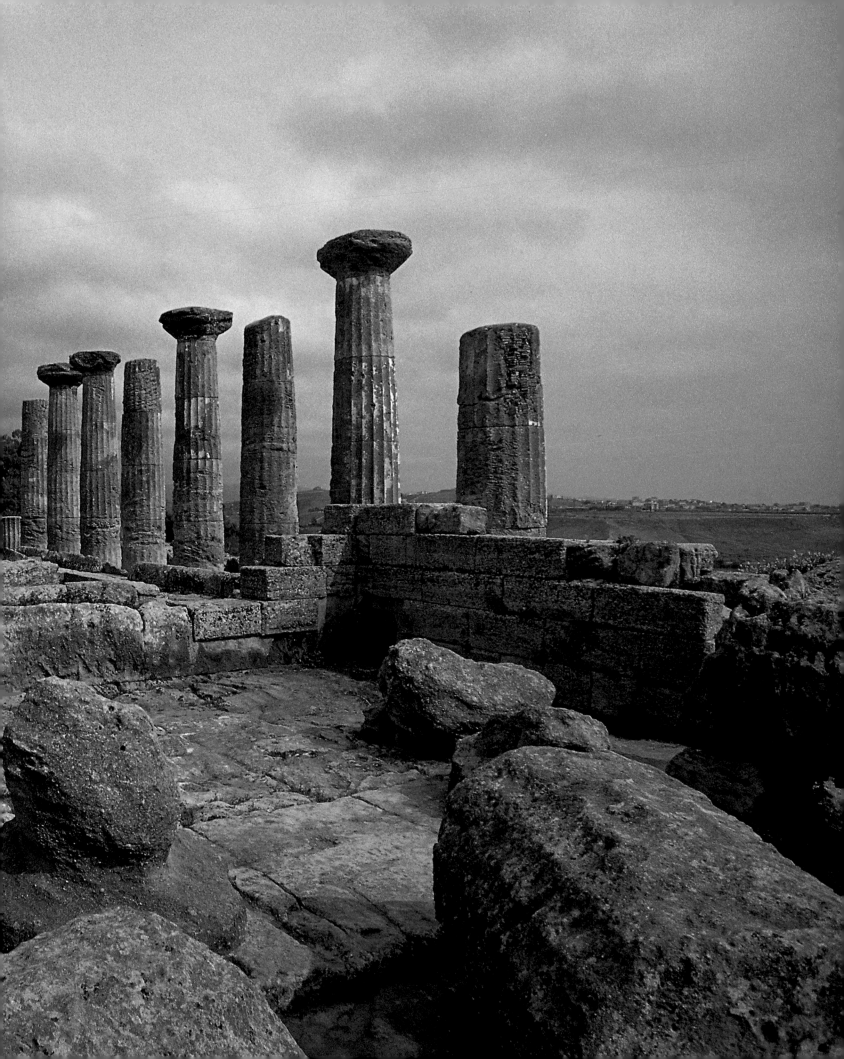

# An Iridescent Fable

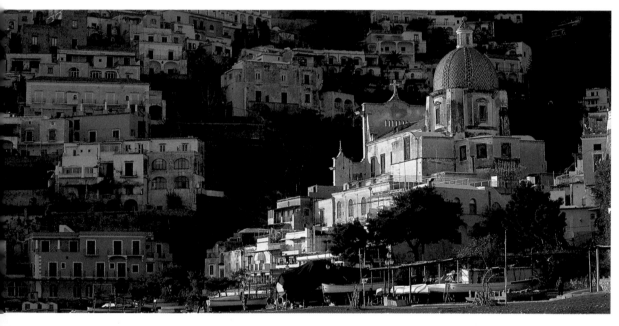

"That which the sea gives, the sea can take away" is an old fisherman's saying. The ancient legends of Scylla and Charybidis and of the sorceress Circe bear witness to the challenge between man and sea. When it was still believed that the Mediterranean was the center of the world and there was nothing else beyond it, the desire for adventure and knowledge moved the spirit of the great navigators, pushing them to undertake voyages which demanded great suffering and dedication. The history of the sea is not only told by the misery of the fishermen who had to fight every day to scrape a living, but also by the riches and power some cities managed to acquire from maritime commerce.

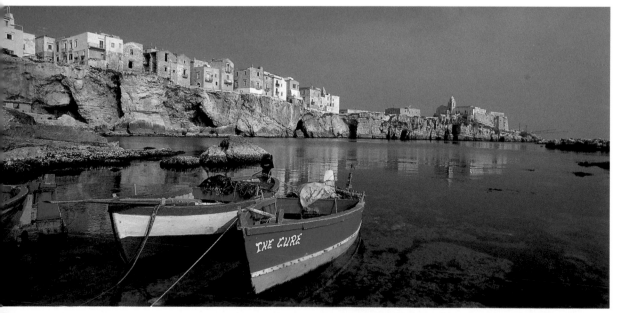

82 top *The old fishing village of Positano is characterized by white houses scattered in picturesque disorder above a small cove on the Amalfi coast.*

82 bottom *On the rocky coast of the Gargano peninsula, which is typified by small coves hidden by pine trees, the town of Vieste is situated on a steep promontory with beaches on either side.*

83 *With its green hills sloping down to the sea, Portofino is one of the most beautiful towns in Liguria.*

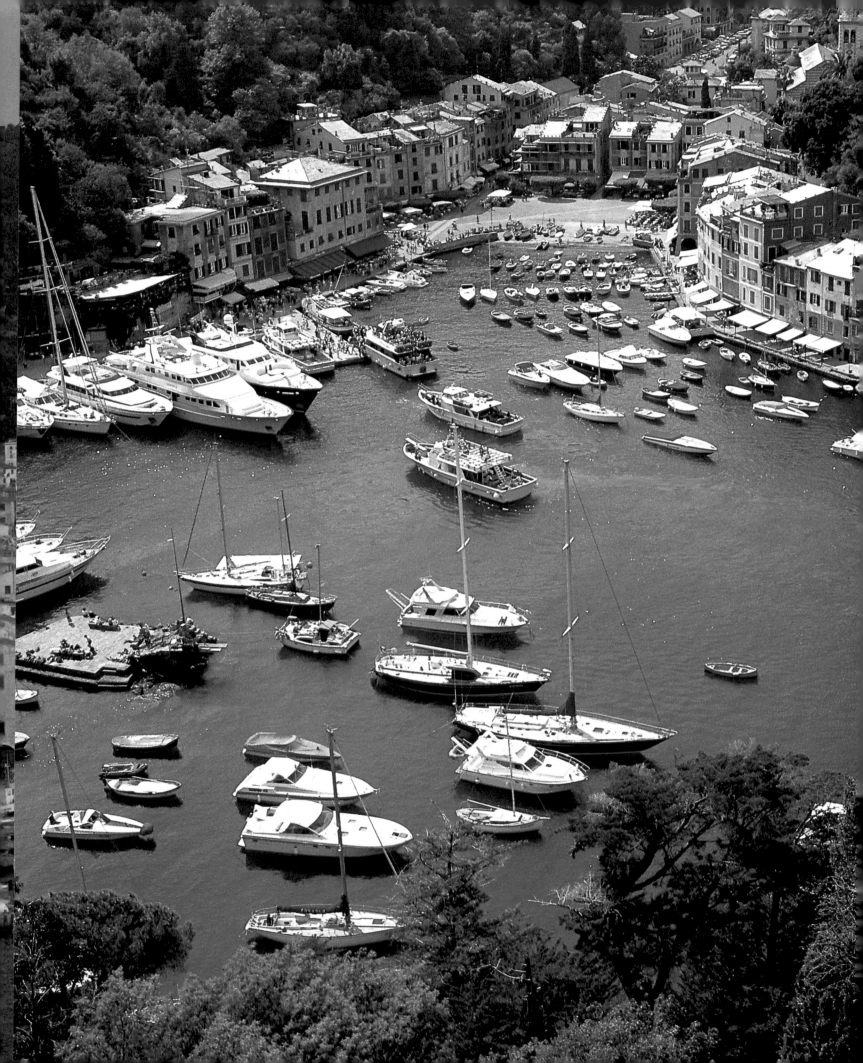

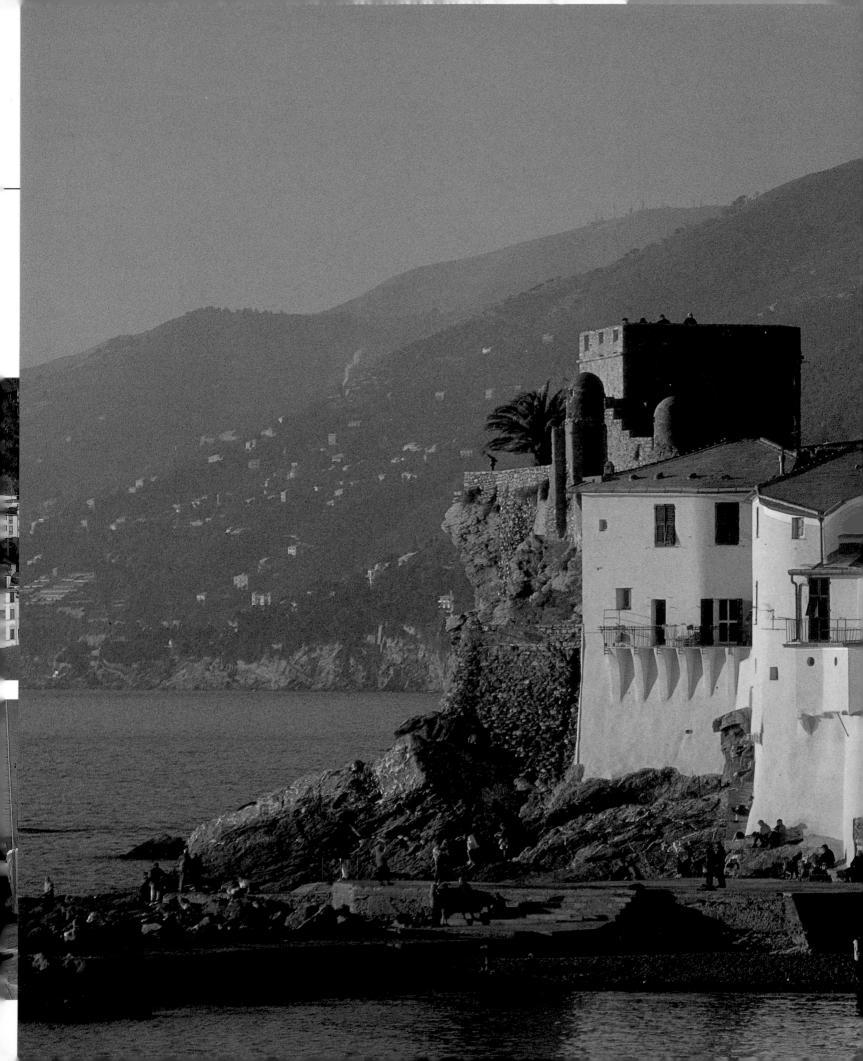

# Cinque Terre: The Relationship Between Man and the Sea

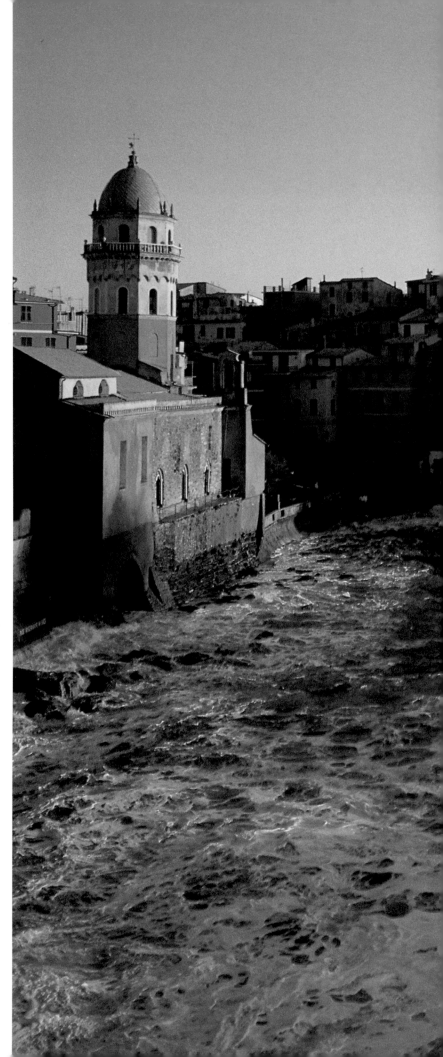

Manarola and Vernazza are two of the five small villages known as the Cinque Terre which nestle at the western end of the Gulf of La Spezia. Until not very long ago, the only means of communication was by sea, rail, or a path which was at times dangerously exposed. Even today the autumnal high seas increase the sense of isolation in these precipitous places.

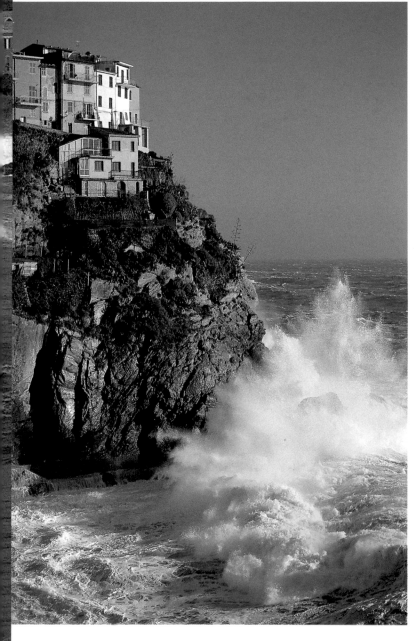

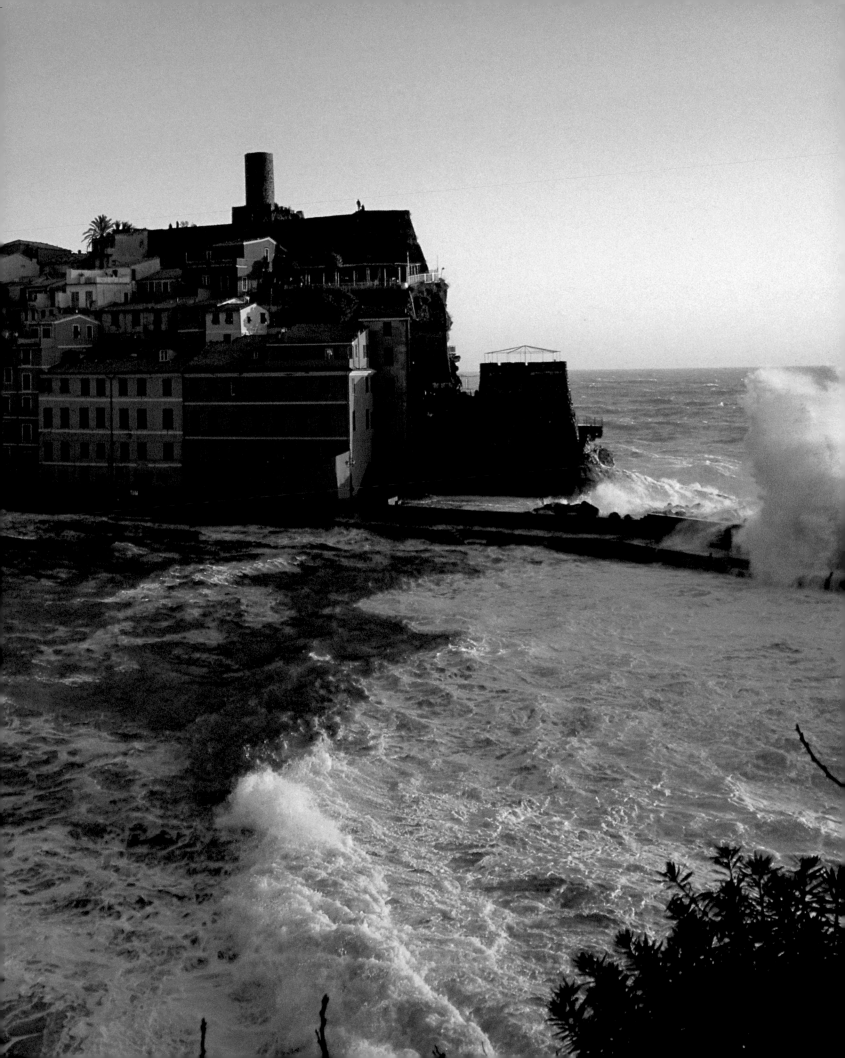

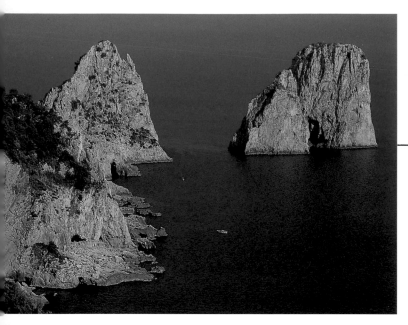

# Island Jewels

Of Italy's smaller islands, Capri is like a precious jewel anchored in an intensely blue sea. Famous among tourists from all over the world, Capri has managed, on the whole, to preserve its natural beauty. The immense calcareous block which forms the island rises out of a deep sea. The island has a jagged and inaccessible coast, which sometimes forms steep cliffs with fantastic profiles or cliffs in which the waves have created dramatic niches and cavities. The most elaborate effects of erosion can be seen in the natural arches or in the romantic Blue Grotto, the sea cave famous for the way light refracts to give it an intense turquoise color.

Although it is not so crowded, the nearby island of Ponza has no cause to be jealous of its more famous neighbor. Here, too, there is the same jagged coastline, crowned by numerous cliffs which highlight a landscape still exciting and wild. The somber and intense color of its rock is similar to the volcanic landscape of the Sicilian island of Lampedusa, the main island in the Pelagi group. White villages stand out clearly in this lunar grayness, as do isolated dwellings surrounded by the meager vegetation—only broom manages to thrive, and its flowers add color in spring. The volcanic rock forms a sharp contrast with the surrounding deep blue crystalline waters. The primordial beauty of the coast has been preserved despite the summer assault of tourists.

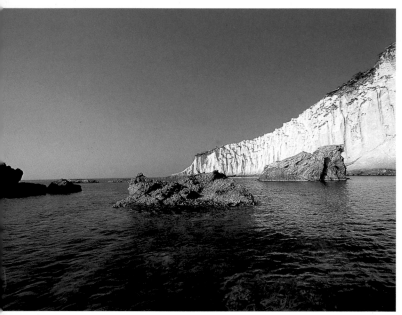

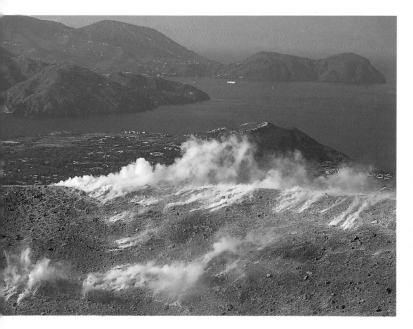

92 top *The famous formations of Capri rise from the depths of the clear blue sea.*

92 center *The island of Ponza has a rugged coastline composed of high walls of multicolored volcanic rock.*

92 bottom *The adventures of Odysseus are recalled in Italy's romantic seascapes.*

93 *The island of Lampedusa, which extends arid and flat over an area of about 20 square kilometers, is the most southerly part of Italy.*

94-95 *Once a penal colony, the island of Capraia in the Tuscan Archipelago is now a nature park.*

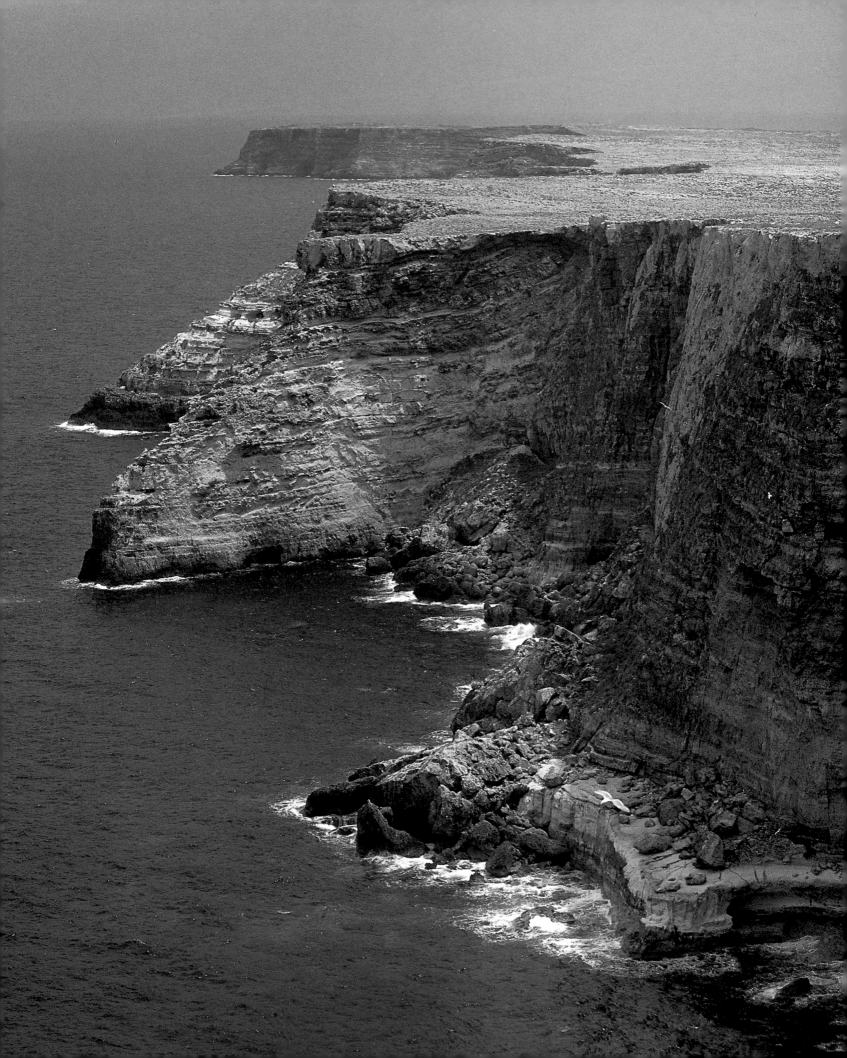

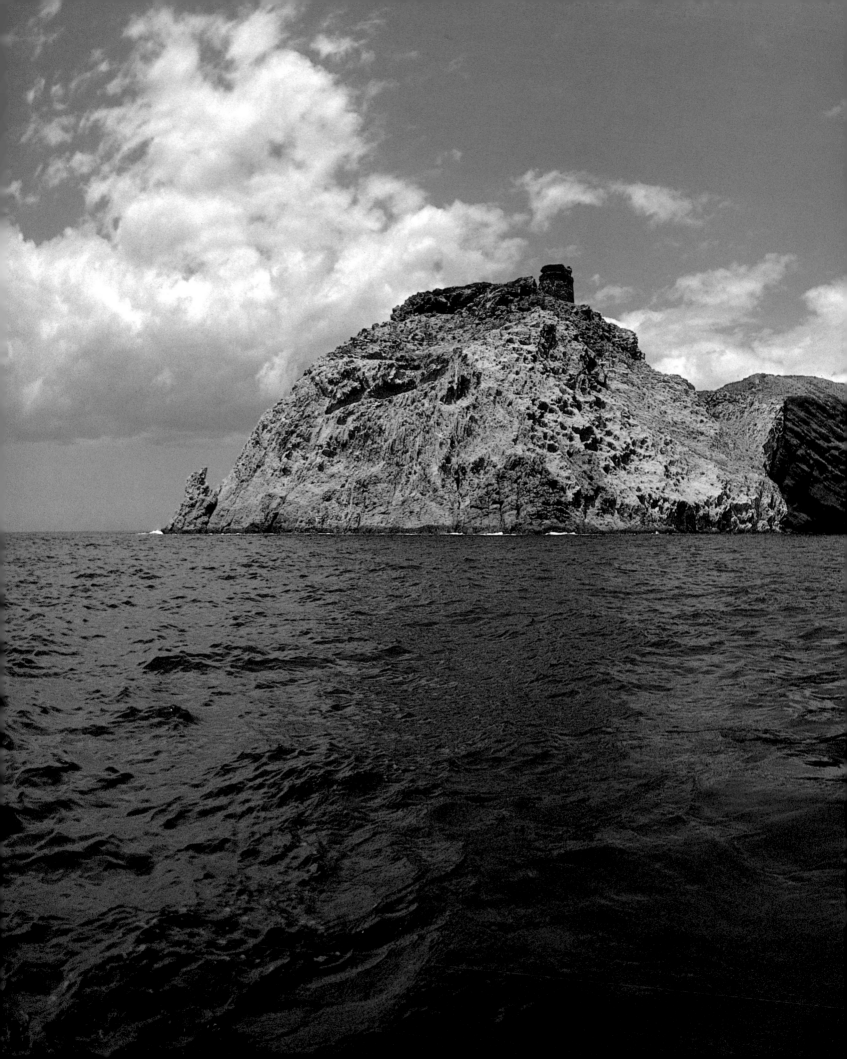

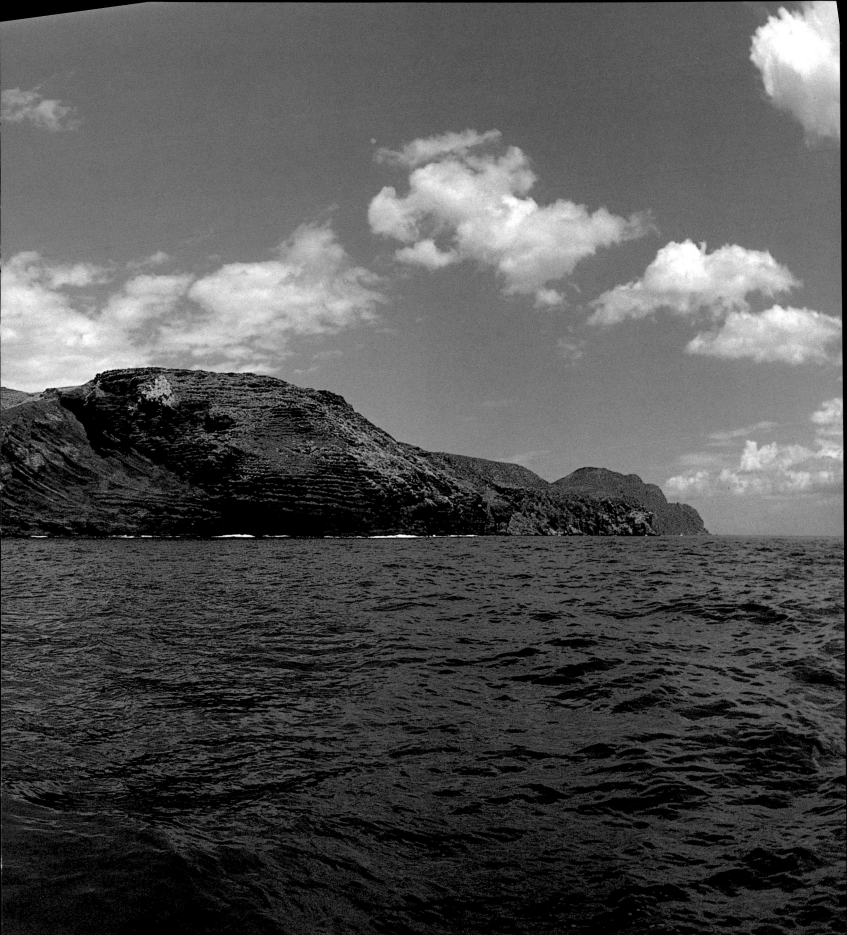

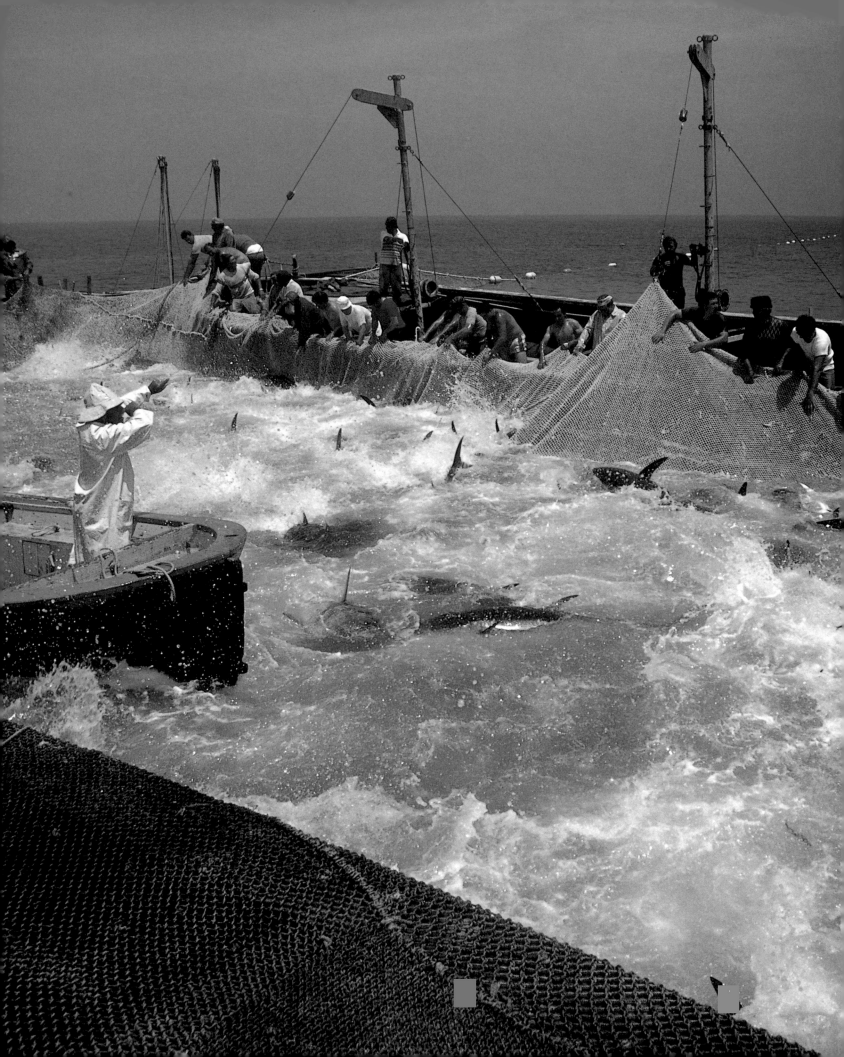

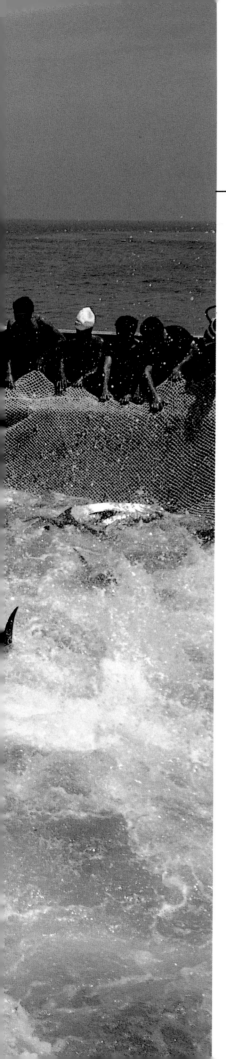

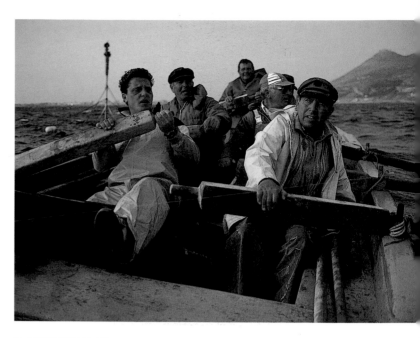

# The Tuna Harvest

The traditional tuna fish slaughter is well-described in Giovanni Verga's novels. A number of vertical nets linked by hawsers tied together to form a T shape are kept afloat with pieces of cork. When the head fisherman, known as the Ràis, gives the order, the net is raised and the slaughter of the fish begins. While singing popular chants, the men haul the stunned

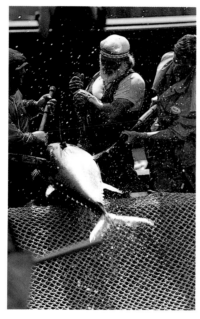

fish on board using long hooks. This maritime tradition is now being replaced by more modern and more lucrative fishing techniques. There are very few people who are prepared to put up with the risks and fatigue involved in this type of fishing. Once the tuna fish slaughter was a social event and a tradition passed on from father to son. Now it is gradually being transformed into a tourist attraction.

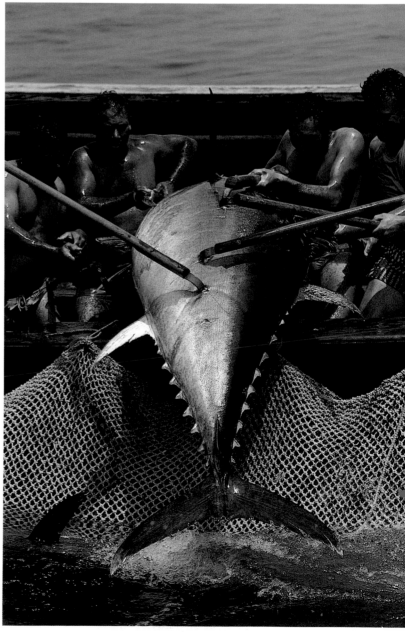

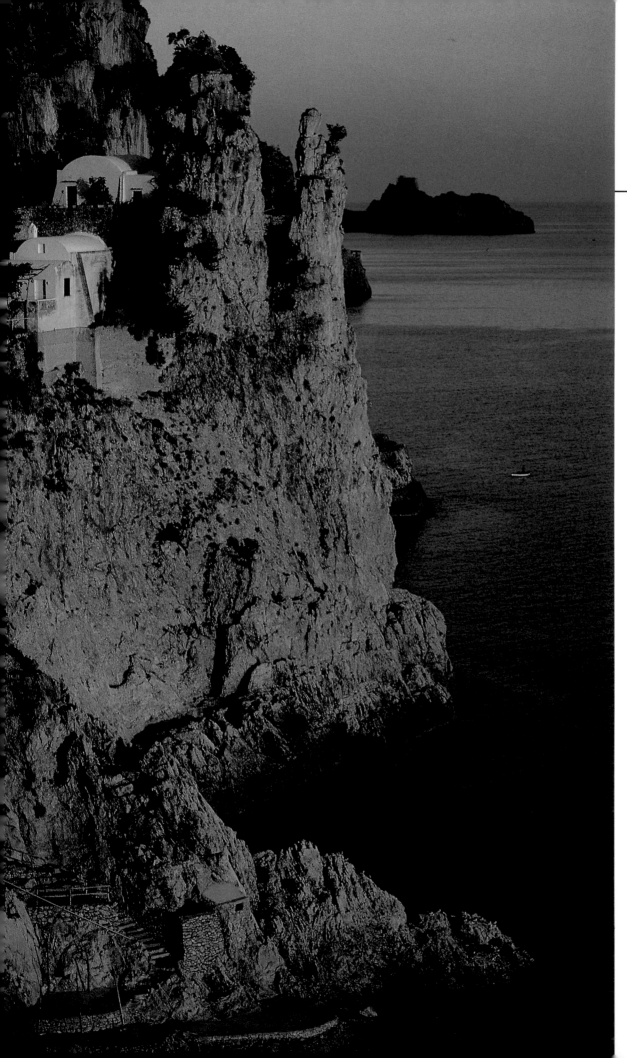

# Wild Beauty Overlooking the Sea

Some of Italy's most rugged coastline comes to an end amid the waves of the Gulf of Salerno and along the coasts of the splendid Pontine Islands where they exhibit their unusual eroded forms. Hidden between the many spurs of rock there are wild ravines and tiny coves which are used by the fishermen to beach their boats. On the rocks are bushes of evergreen plants and hedges of prickly pears. A large number of terraces, held up by high walls and the patient toil of man, are planted with olives, vines, and oranges, each with its particular shade of green. In this setting, the houses of the fishermen, with their warm, sunny colors, fit in harmoniously.

98 *The precipitous rocks, steep crags, and deep gorges of the Amalfi Coast have earned it universal fame.*

99 *Ventonone is characterized by the typical stucco houses of this lovely village on the island of the same name in the Pontine Archipelago.*

100-101 *Nestled between the mountains and the sea, Amalfi forms an image of lively and evocative beauty.*

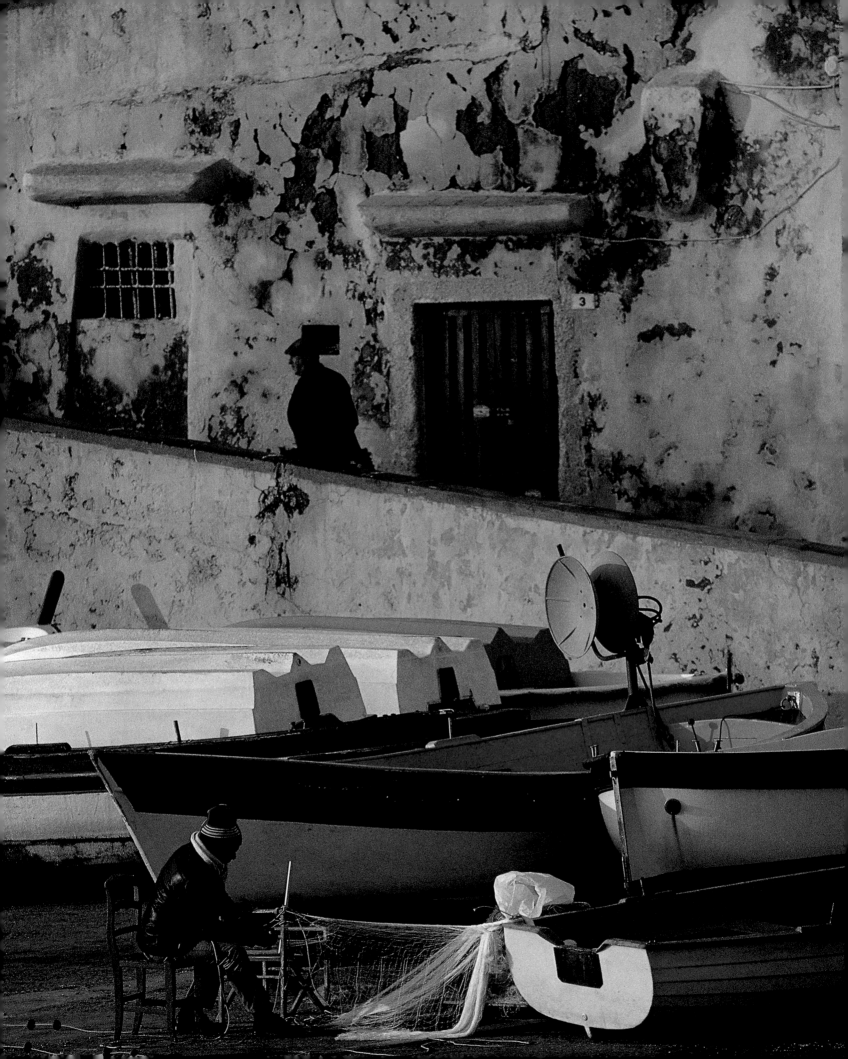

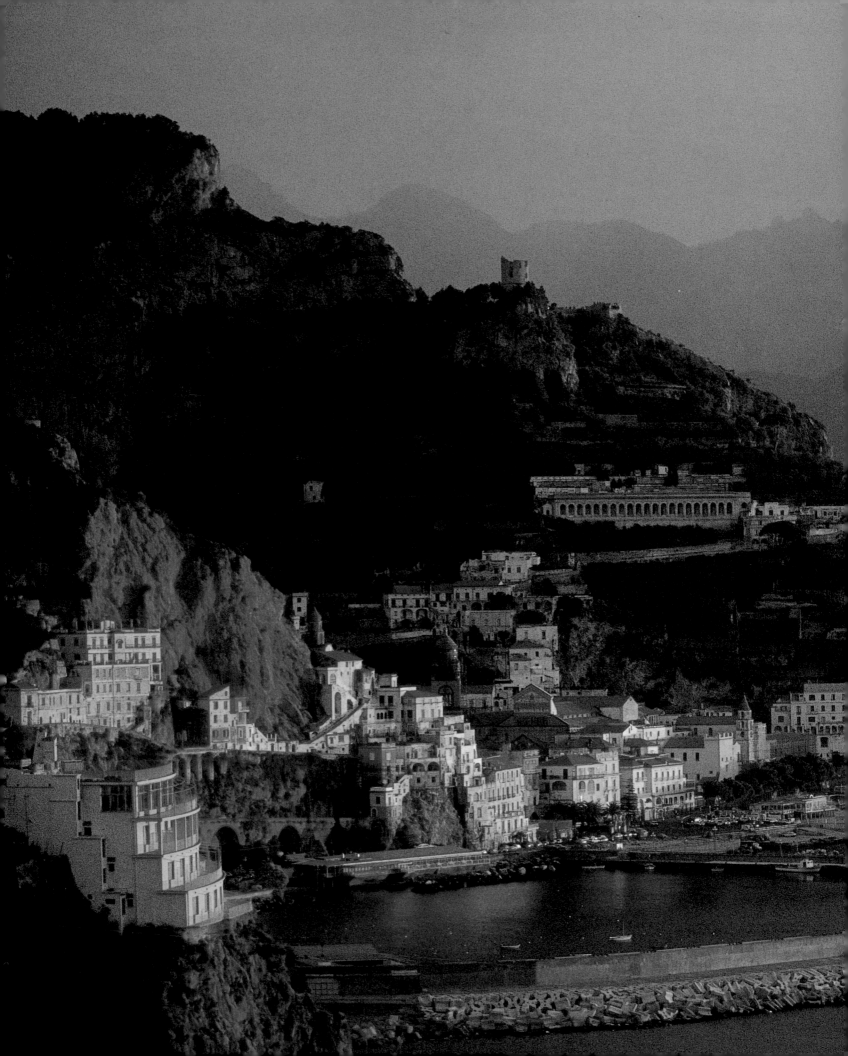

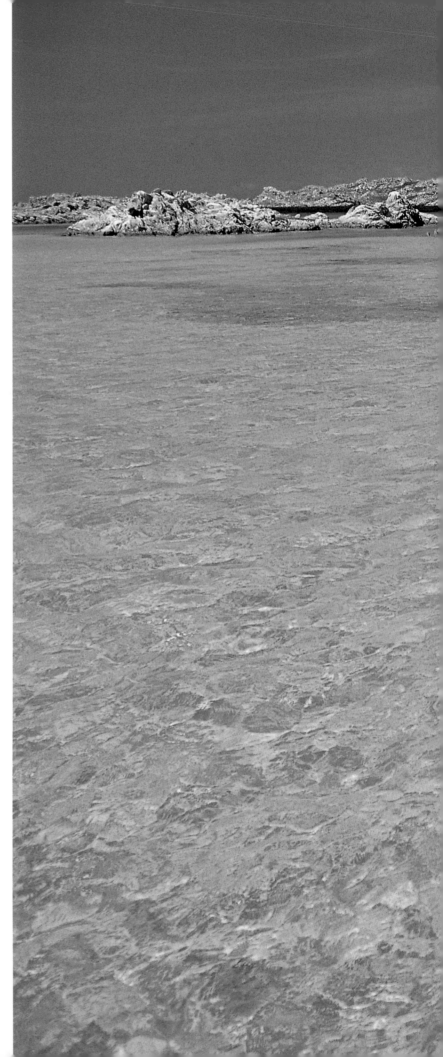

# Sardinia,
# Land of Colors
# and Contrasts

*102-103 In the small island of Budelli, nature has skillfully mixed its colors: green waters, pink beaches, and tenacious vegetation give this coastline an unparalleled charm.*

*104-105 The lookout tower at Stintino, mysterious sentinel of a forgotten past, stands out against the intense blue of the sea.*

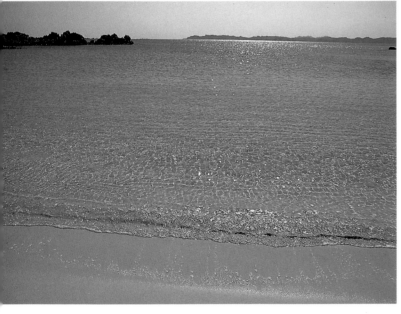

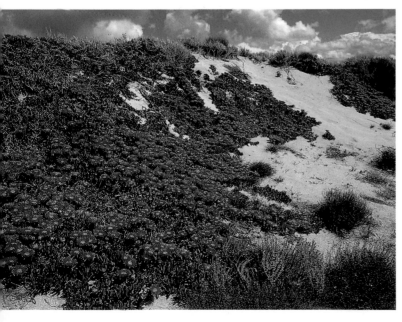

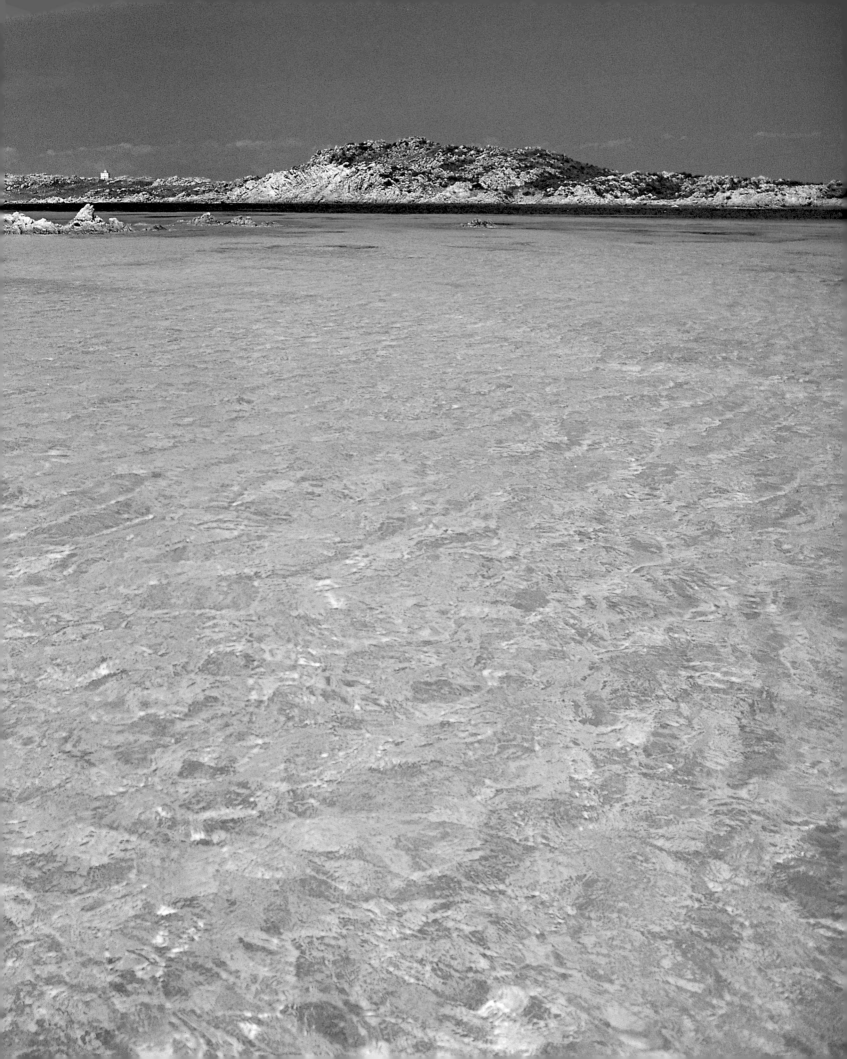

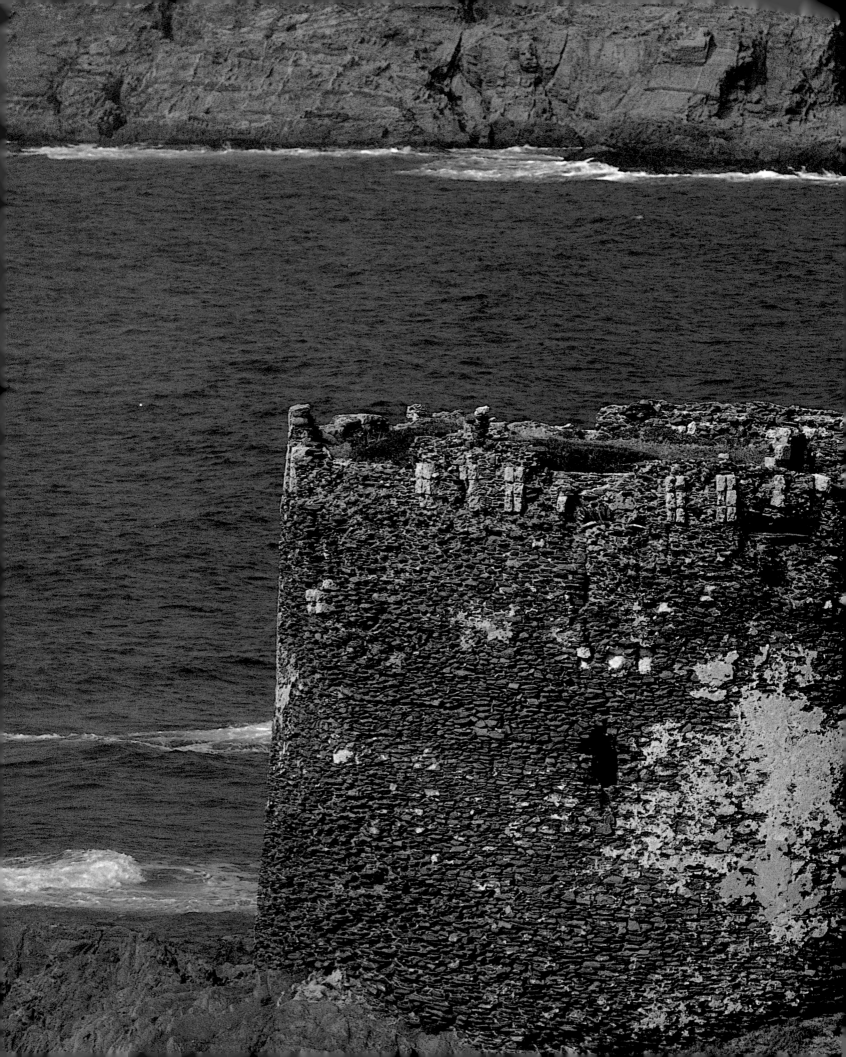

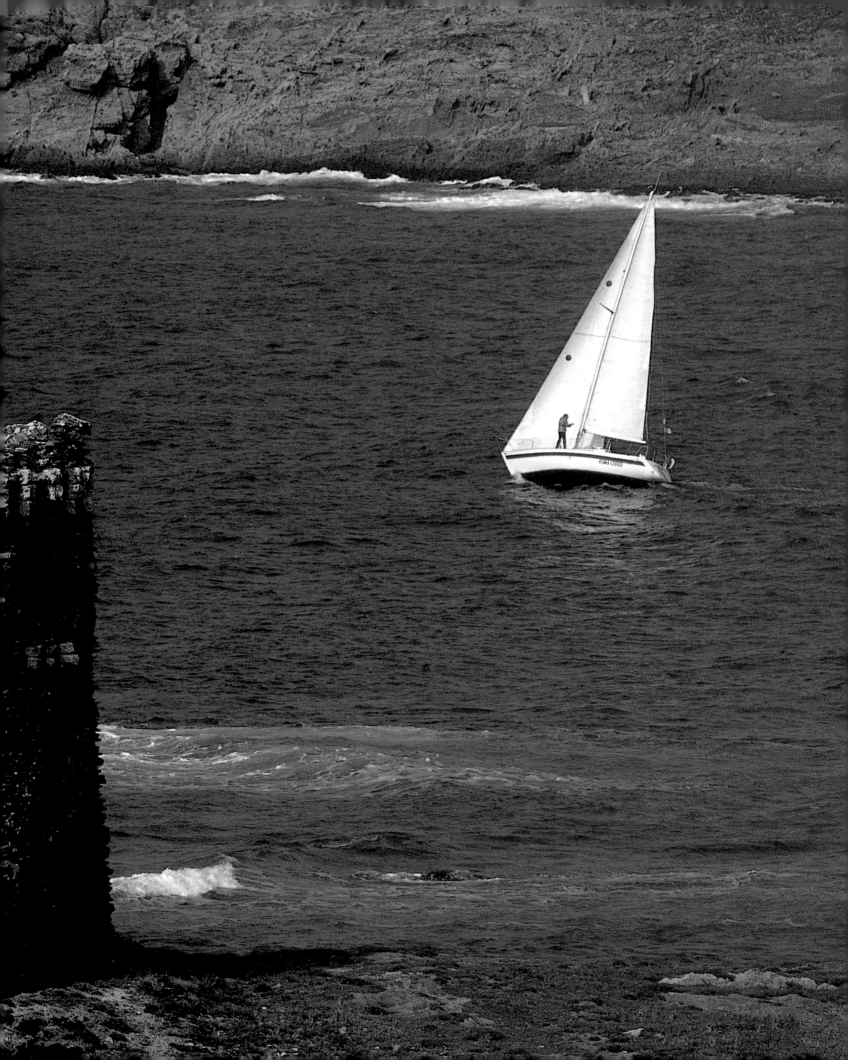

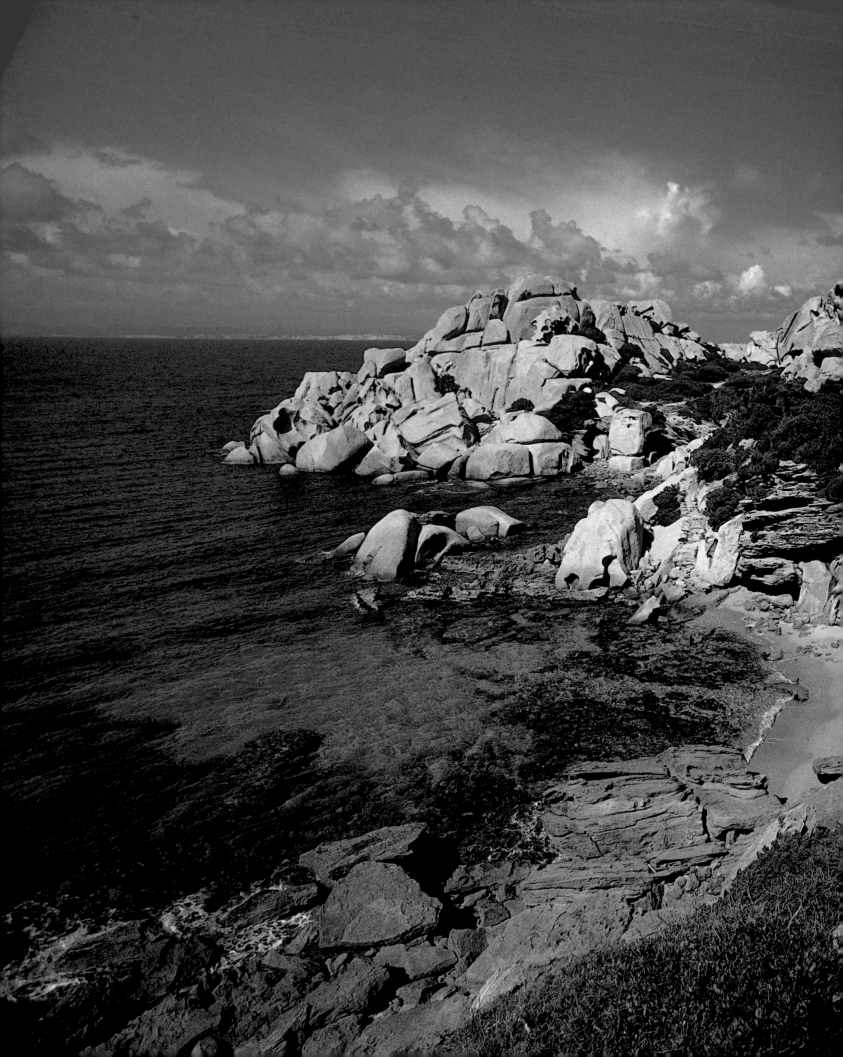

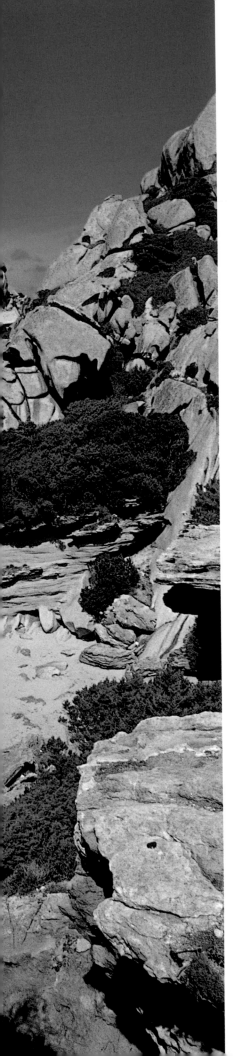

The coastal landscape of Sardinia displays an amazing variety of forms as a result of the sea's erosive force. At the edge of the sea, the waves batter the rock; in the inlets, the coast reveals the entire range of its colors, from somber to bright. High mountains fall steeply into a sea whose colors range from green to turquoise, and the imposing granitic formations slope down more gently, constantly modeled by the action of the waves.

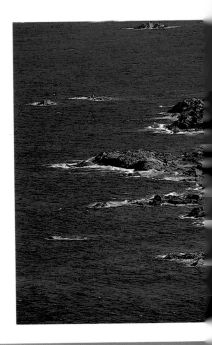

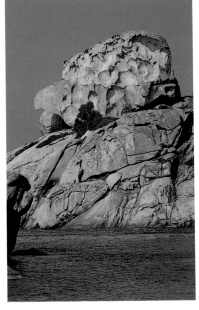

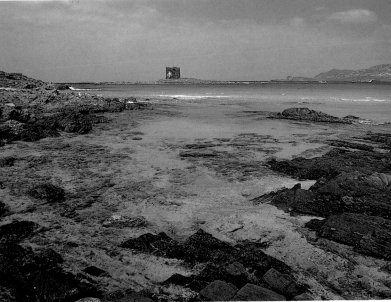

106-107 *Capo Testa, situated in the north of the island, is one of the most interesting natural areas in Sardinia.*

107 top *The rugged spurs of the northern coast of the island of La Maddelena extend into the sea.*

107 left *Hollowed by the action of sea and wind, the rocks of the Sardinian coast reflect the variety of the island's forms and colors.*

107 center *The color of the sea at Stintino seems even more extraordinary because of its contrast with the white beach.*

107 bottom *With variations in light and weather, the sea around Sardinia constantly takes on new shades and a different character.*

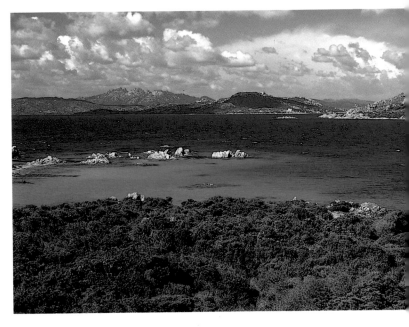

# The Mountains:
# Enormous Sentries

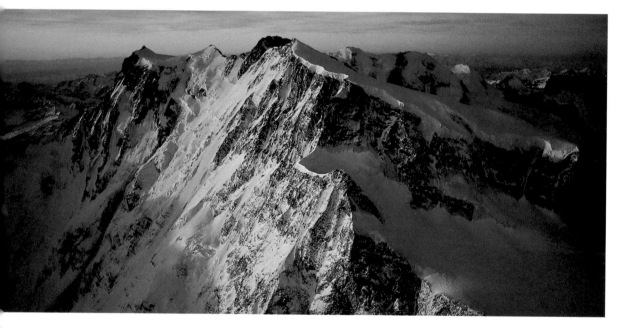

The imposing Alpine arc, guardian of northern Italy, contains the highest European peaks and constitutes one of the most important geographical features of the country. Soaring, windswept summits, dazzling white glaciers, desolate stretches of morainic scree, rugged rocky valleys and verdant ones, raging torrents and peaceful lakes glittering like gems form the magnificent landscape in which man has left his imprint. Path signs, shepherds' huts, and chapels remind us of the hard work and dedication of the mountain people who continue to pass on their archaic traditions. For these people, the Alps are something more than a training ground for sports.

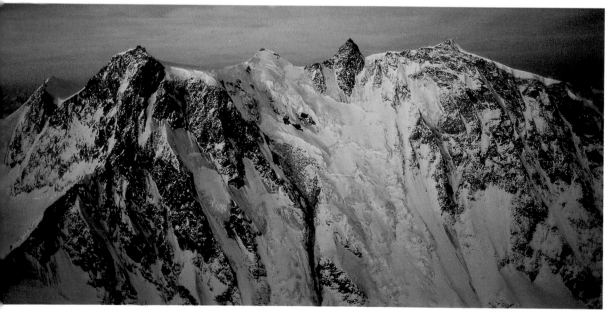

108-109 *The Monte Rosa Group in the Pennine Alps got its name from the fact that its snow-covered peaks take on a pink glow at dawn and sunset.*

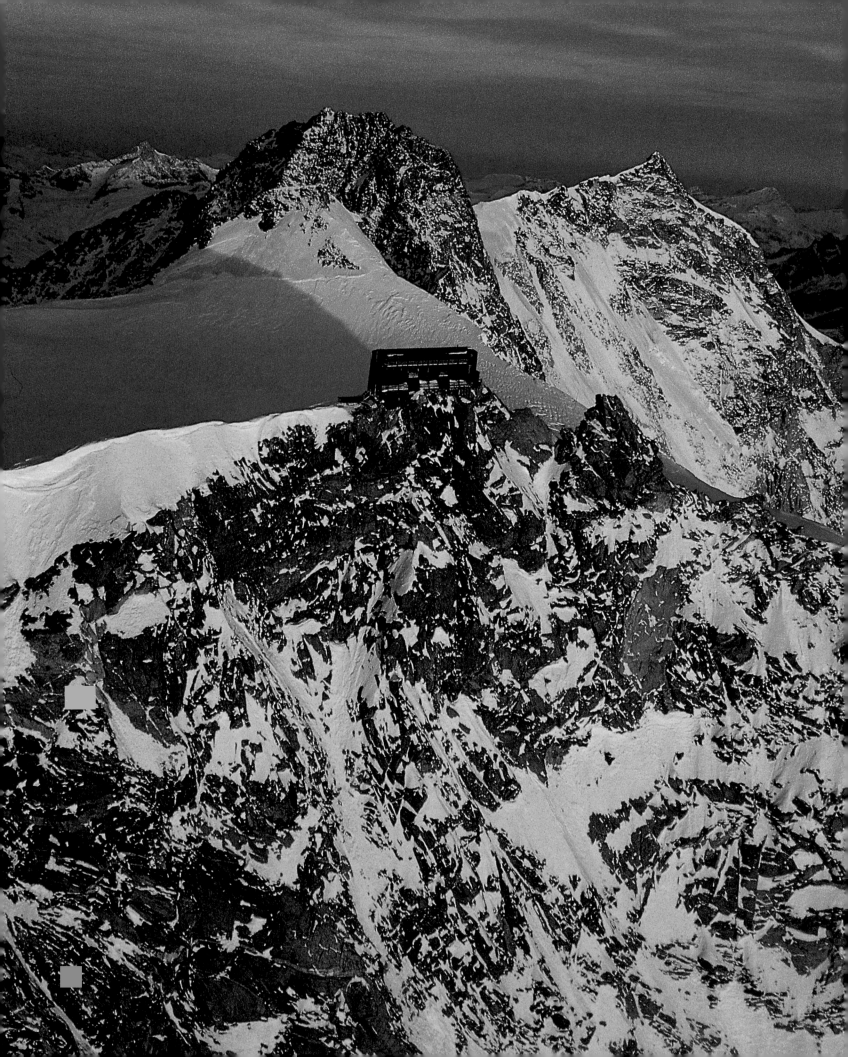

# The Alps, Sentinels of Italy

110 top *Les Grandes Jorasses form part of the Mont Blanc massif.*

110 bottom *Mont Blanc reaches a height of 4,810 meters.*

110-111 *The distinctive pyramid of the Matterhorn towers over the surrounding peaks.*

112-113 *The Dente del Gigante is one of the most difficult summits in the Mont Blanc massif.*

114-115 *The Alps offer striking panoramas of peaks and glaciers.*

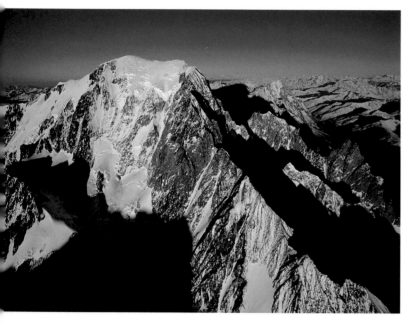

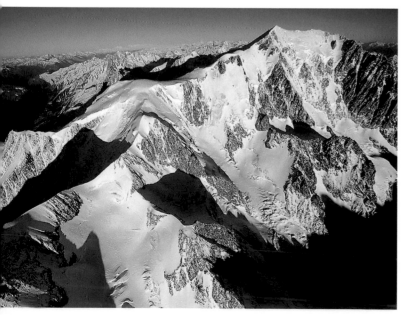

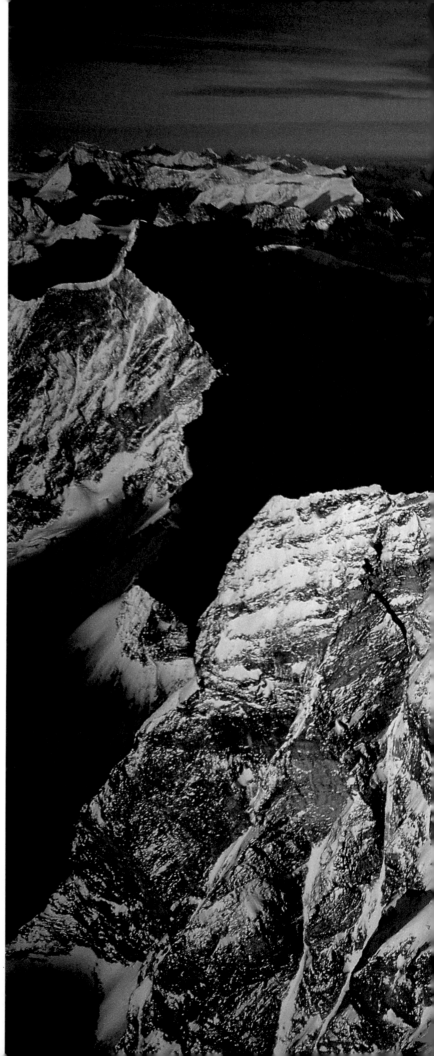

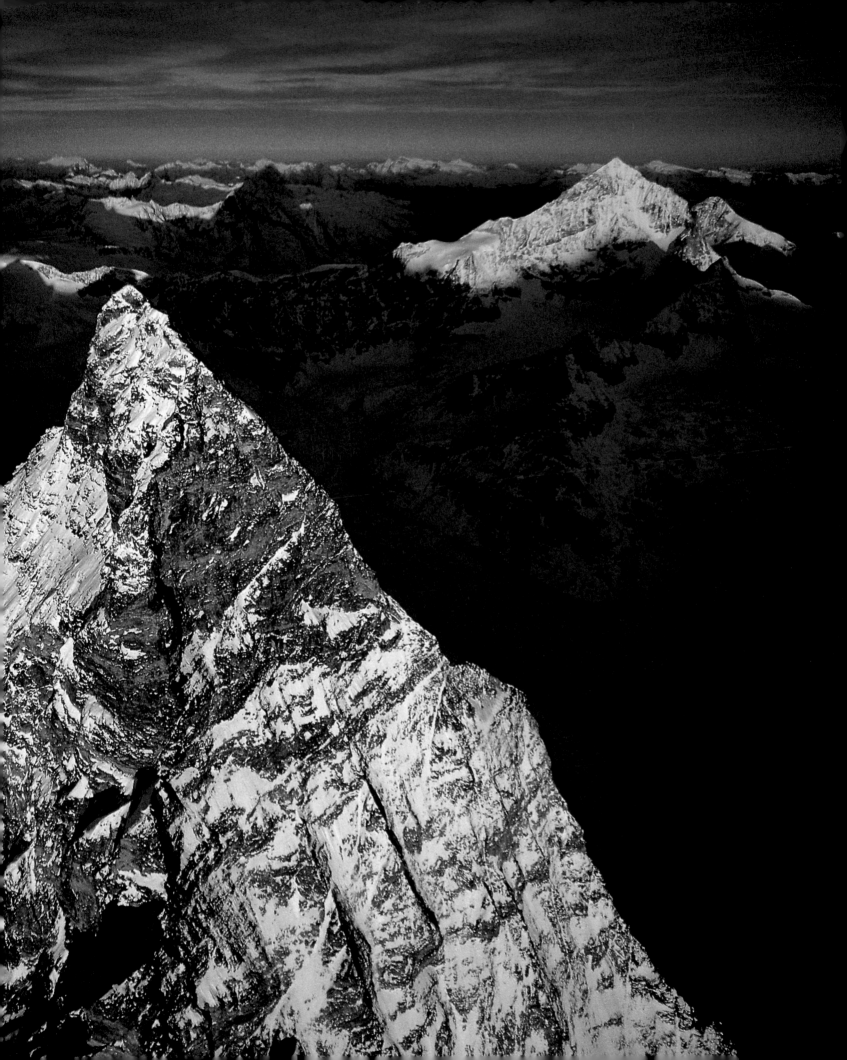

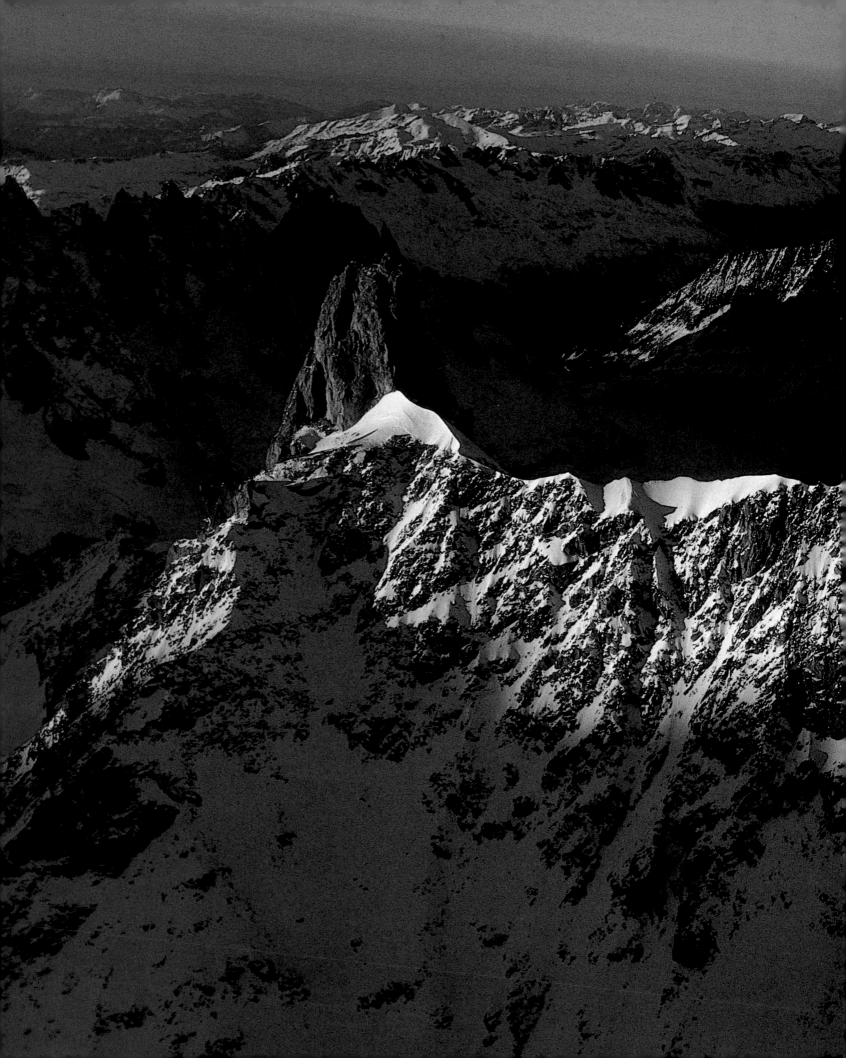

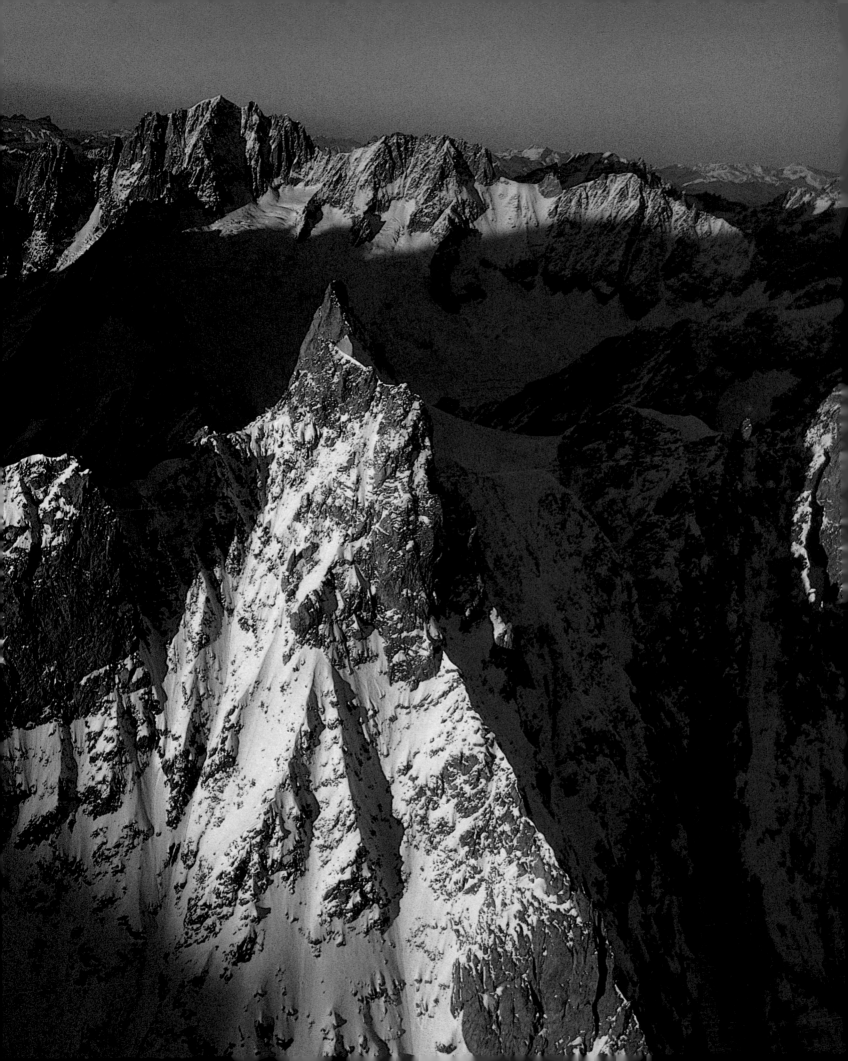

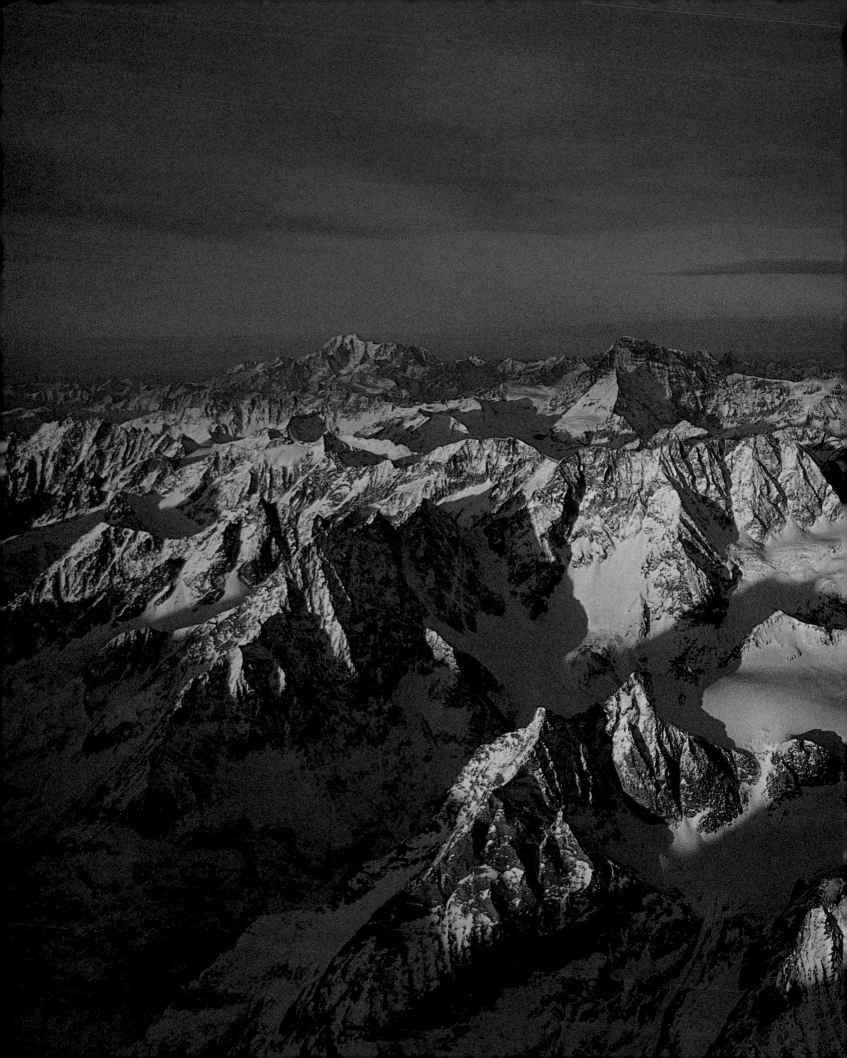

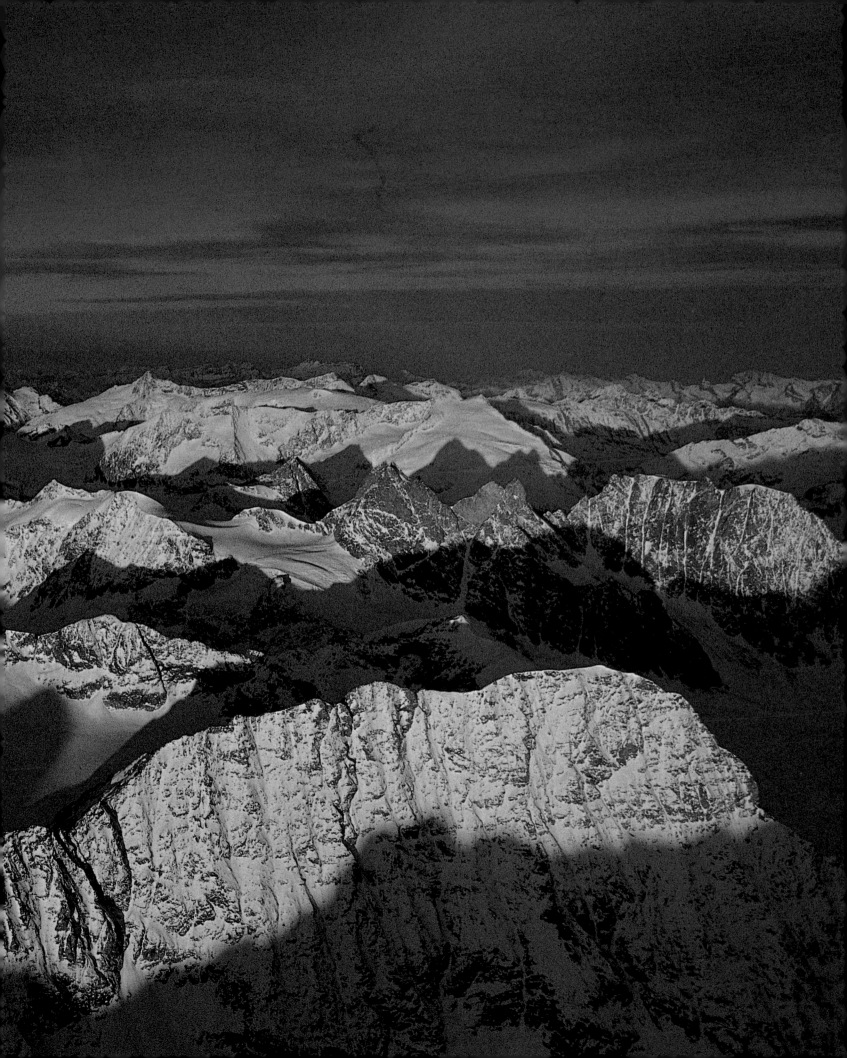

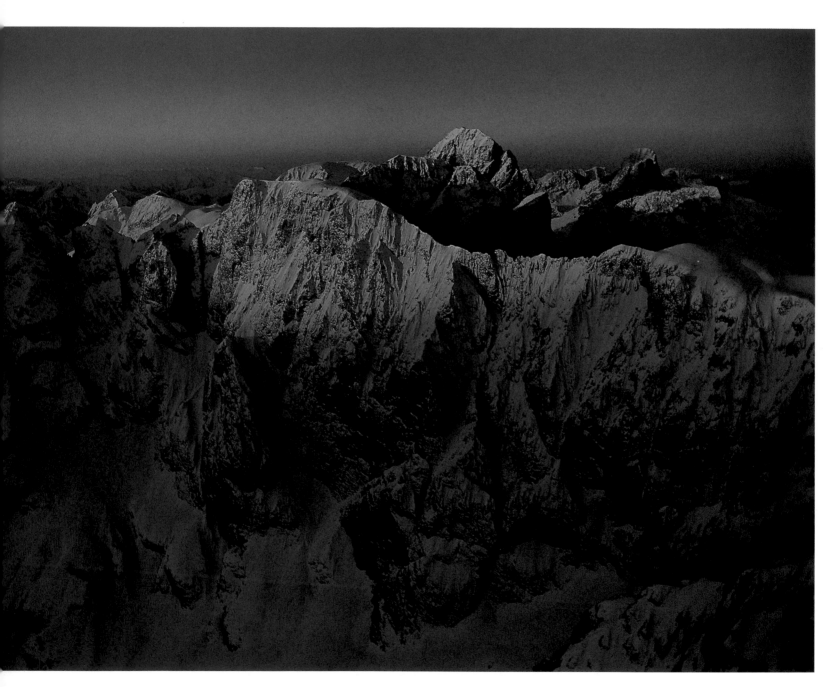

116 *The Torri del Vaiolet is part of the Catinaccio Group in the Dolomite range.*

117 *The Brenta Dolomites, to the west of the River Adige, have a rich mountaineering history which began around 1880.*

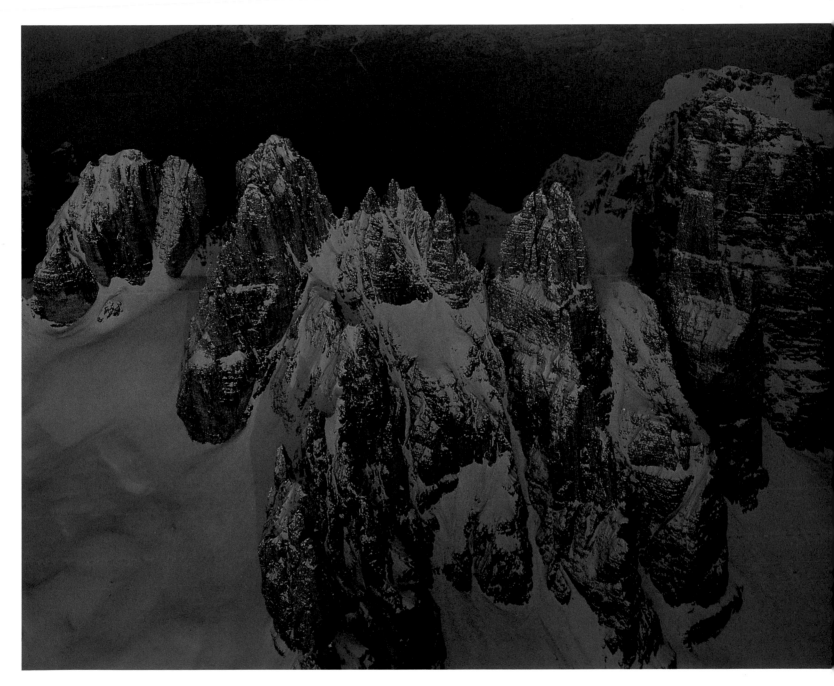

118-119 *The Sella Group towers over the four surrounding valleys of Ladine like an immense monolith.*

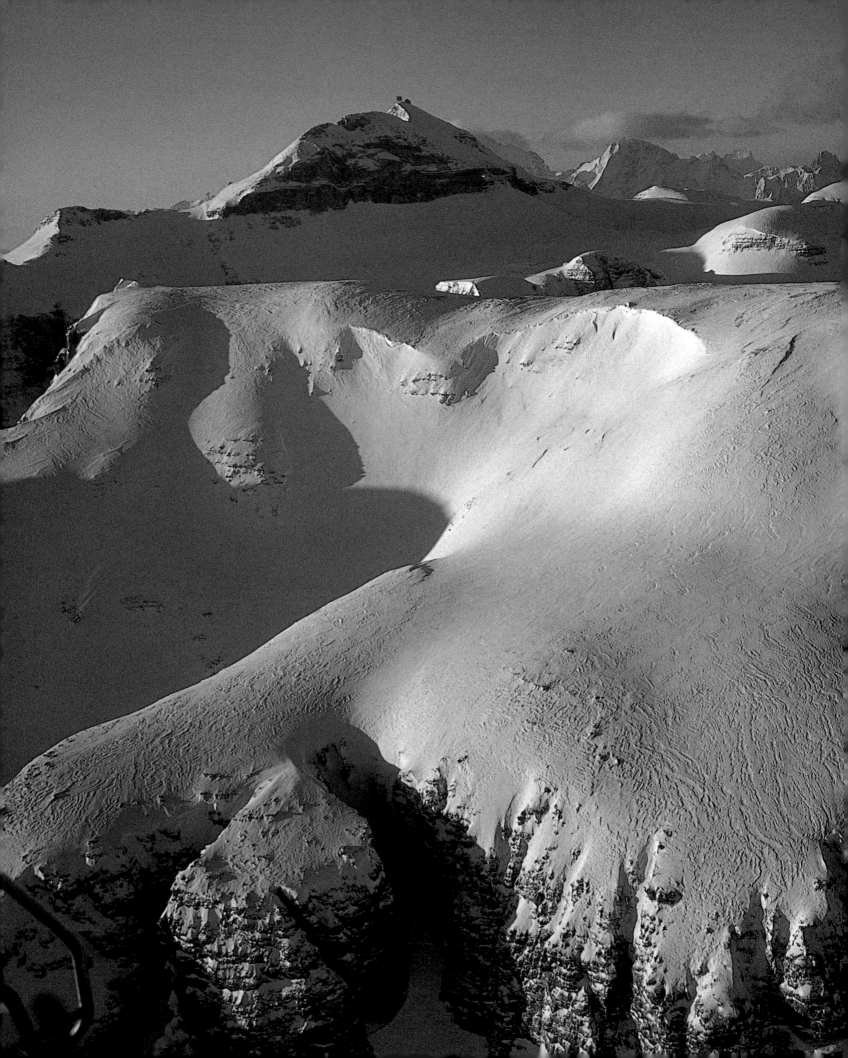

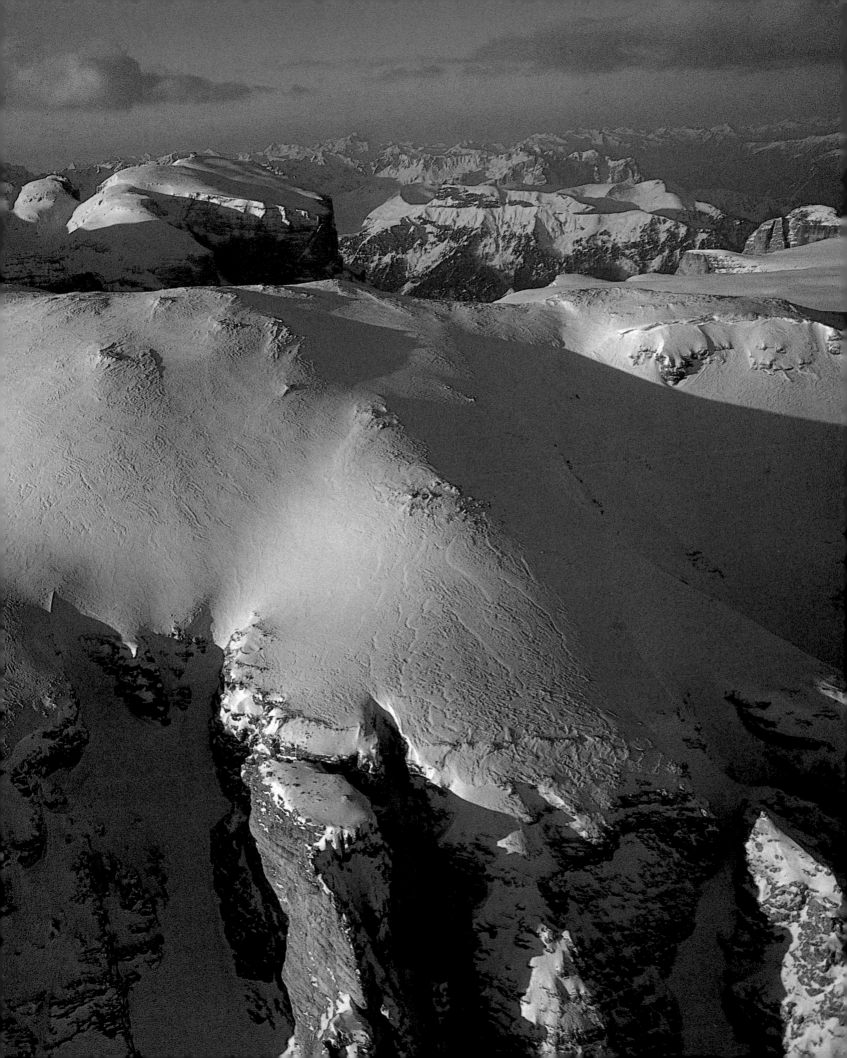

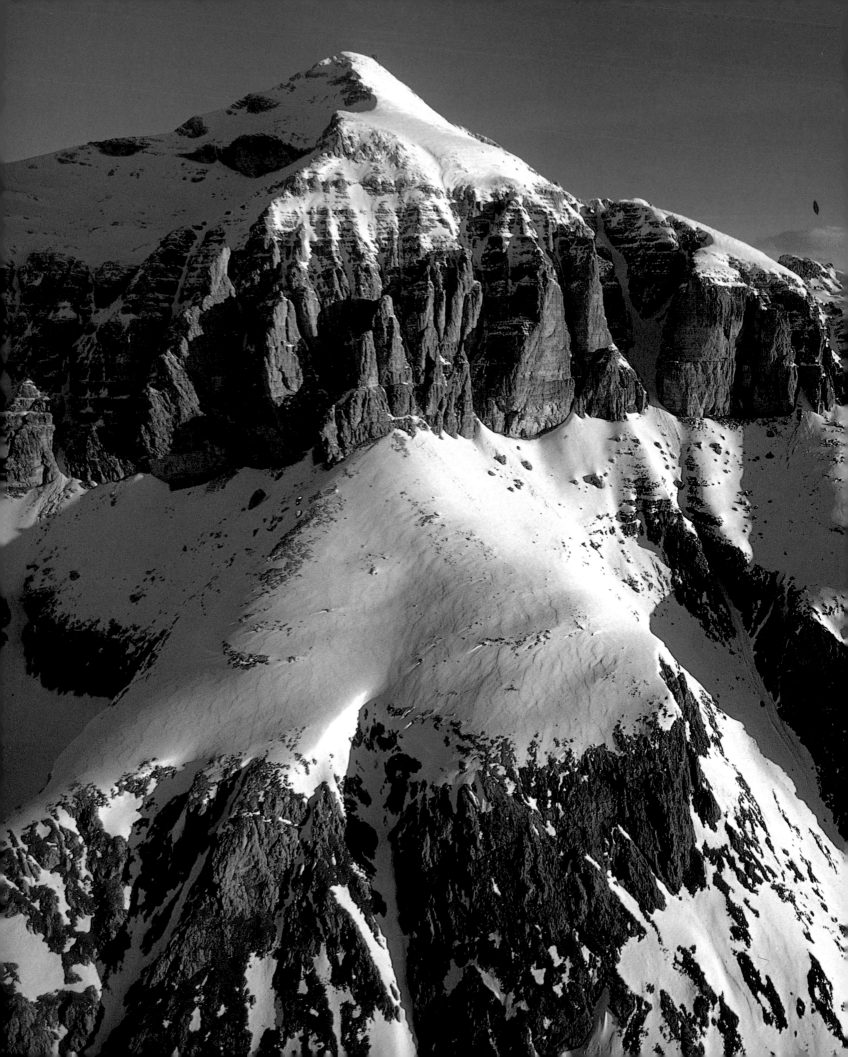

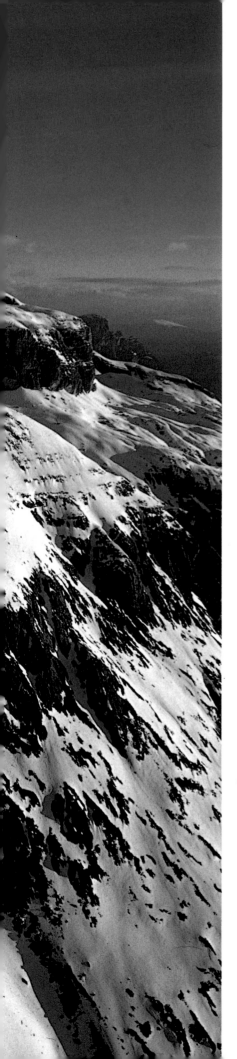

The high rock walls and craggy summits of the Dolomites resemble the fanciful ruins of immense castles. Unlike the granitic Alpine ranges, the large calcareous masses of the Dolomite peaks are clearly distinct and separate from each other, forming clearly defined groups. The range has always been a challenge to mountaineers who must use special climbing techniques to scale the peaks. The deep pink of the dolomite rock contrasts dramatically with the green forests and pastures which slope down to form the valley, studded here and there with small lakes. The flora of the Pale Mountains is among the richest in the entire Alpine arc, and is best represented by the yellow Rhaetian poppy.

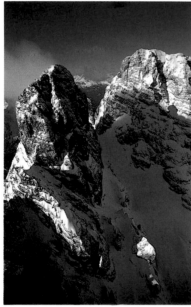

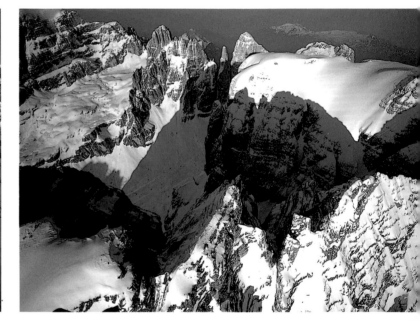

120-121 *The Sella massif consists of a single block of rock which can be reached only after crossing meadows, woods, scree, and rock faces. The Sella group rises from a vast plateau from which also emerges the peak of Piz Boé.*

121 top left and right *The rock and ice of the Dolomites provide challenges to mountaineers from all over the world. Bruno Detassis, who currently runs the Bruntei mountain hut, is the undisputed king of the Brenta Dolomites.*

121 bottom *The Rozes peak in the Tofane Group dominates the basin of Cortina D'Ampezzo.*

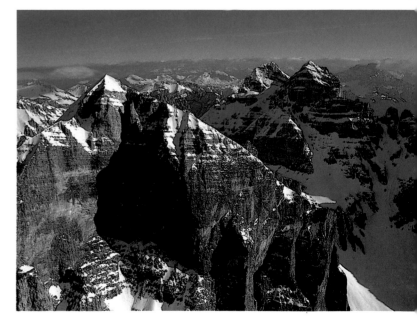

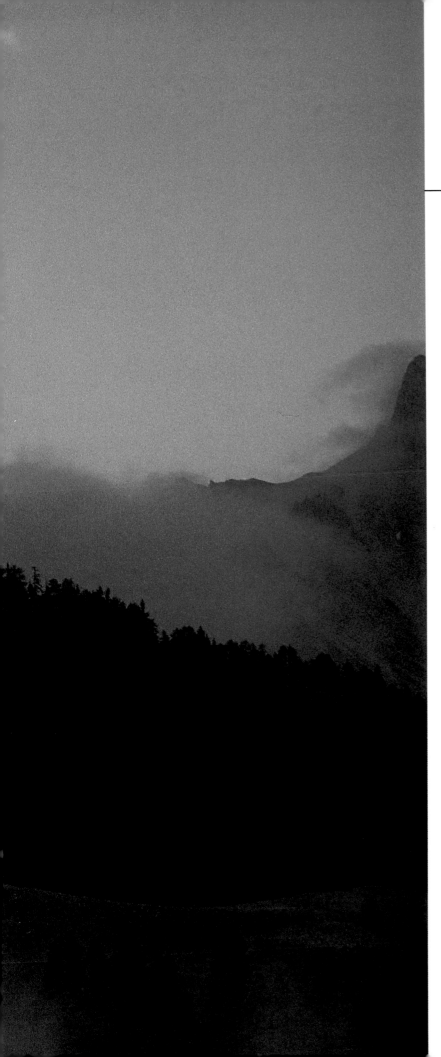

# Memories of Life's Ancient Rhythms: Val Badia

The Val Badia is inhabited by a minority of Ladins who continue to speak a dialect of neo-Latin origin. The costumes and customs of this ethnic group of artisans and farmers have survived intact through the years. Local settlements known as "vilas," hamlets consisting of between six and twenty houses, still survive in this valley.

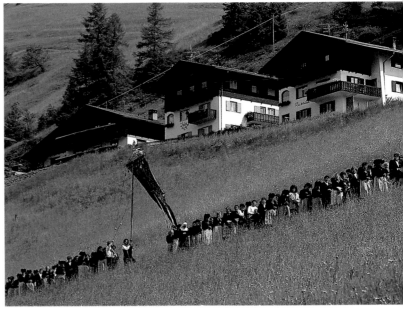

122-123 *The natural beauty of Val Badia offers breathtaking views which have always attracted tourists.*

123 *The residents of Val Badia gather each year for a procession in honor of the Sacred Heart of Jesus.*

# The Sibylline Mountains

The Sibylline Mountains conjure up memories of ancient rites and mysterious legends. According to legend, Sibyl's cavern was located among these heights, where an enchanted world filled with inestimable treasures opened up at the end of a deep grotto. Today these mountains, crisscrossed by deep gorges and steep gullies, still provide habitat for wolves and wildcats, golden eagles and peregrine falcons. The slopes are sometimes softened by a blanket of snow in winter; in spring the meadows are covered with wildflowers. Nestled in the valley or perched on solitary mountain crests, these tiny villages still hand down all the marvels of a world which has changed very little. Even today, an encounter with fairies seems more than just a figment of the imagination.

124-125 *The old hamlet of Castelluccio, standing out against the snowy mass of Mount Vettore, is the highest in the Sibylline Mountains.*

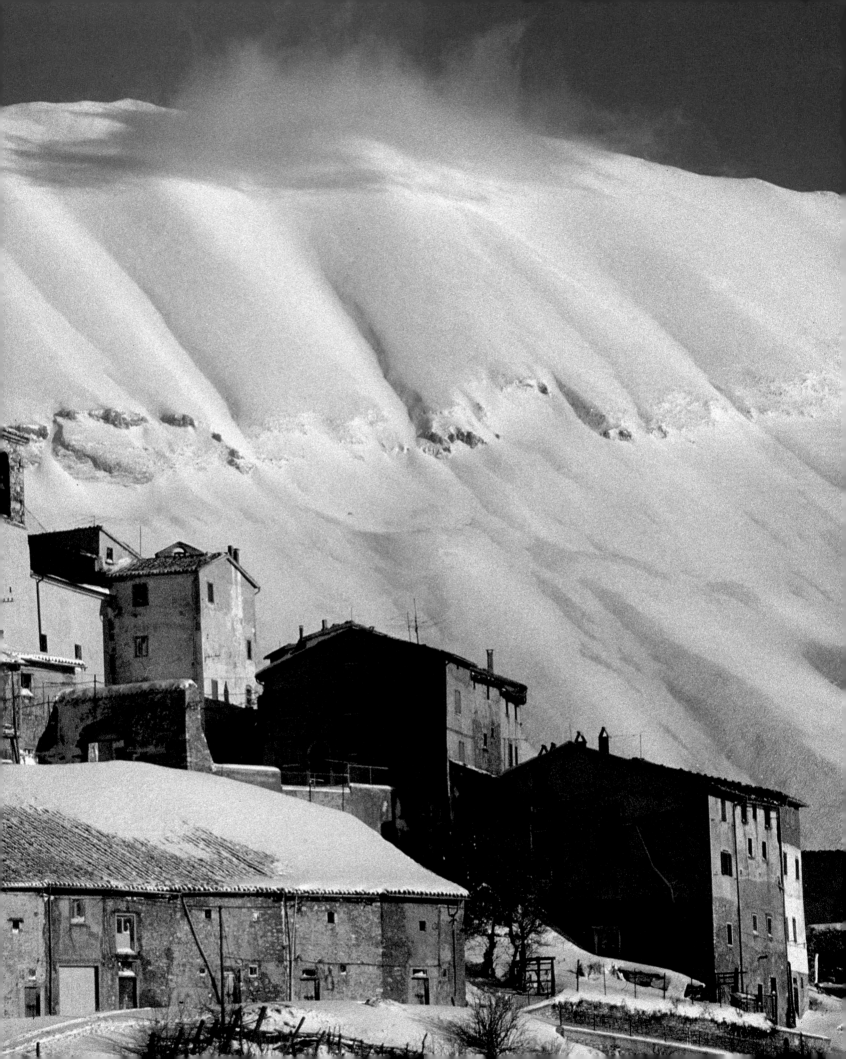

# In the Mouth of the Volcano

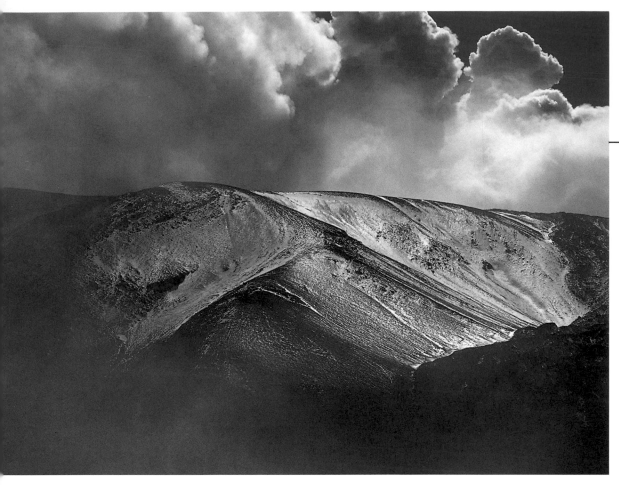

According to a myth, Vulcan was the lord of fire and metal forging. With the help of the Cyclops he worked in the hidden recesses of Mt. Etna. Recalling the ancient legend, Mt. Etna dominates the Sicilian landscape, offering views of unrivaled beauty. It is the largest volcano in Europe, with its central crater at a height of over 3,000 meters. The precipitous Bove Valley cuts deep into the mountainside, and 250 craters formed by lateral eruptions scar its surface. Over the millennia, its activity has created a unique environment and has always challenged those who have stubbornly faced the continuous danger of eruptions to settle on its fertile slopes. There are other volcanoes on the islands; Stromboli has a single crater which is more or less in constant activity.

126 top *The imposing cone of Mt. Etna rises along Sicily's eastern coast.*

126 bottom *Nocturnal excursions to the Stromboli volcano are very popular with tourists who visit this island.*

127 *With a guide, the more adventurous may still observe up close the awesome sight of lava erupting from one of Etna's numerous craters.*

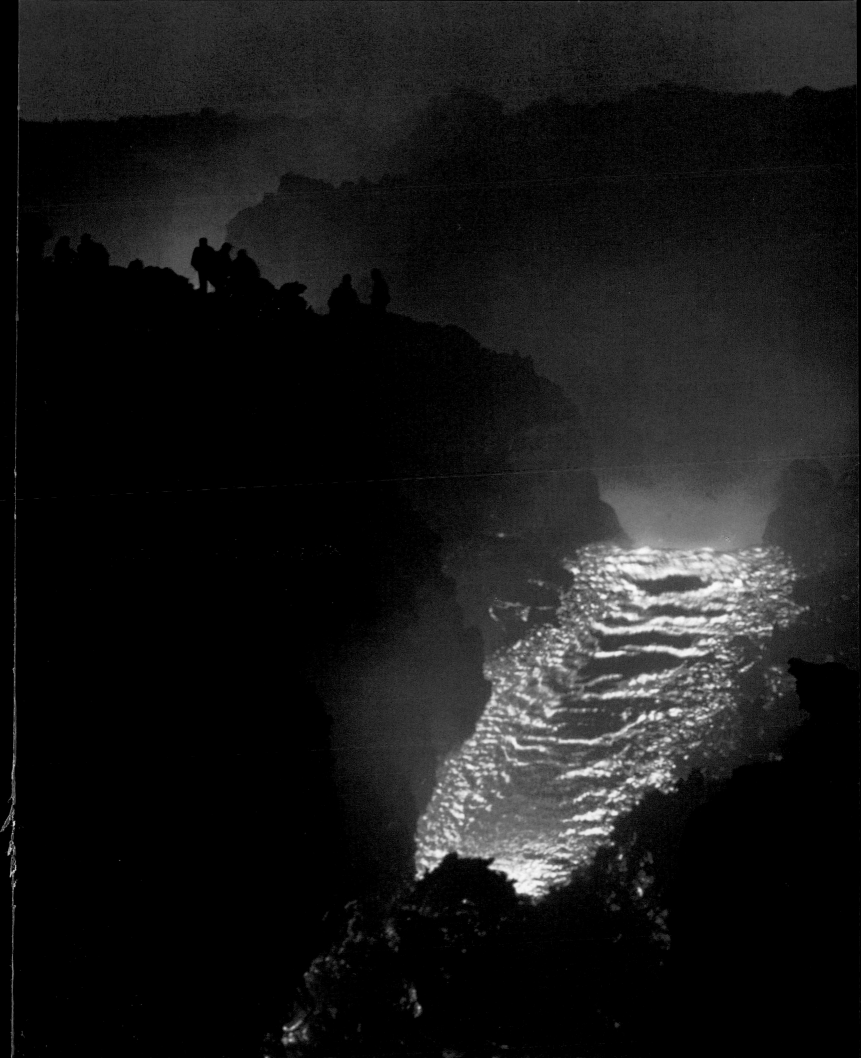

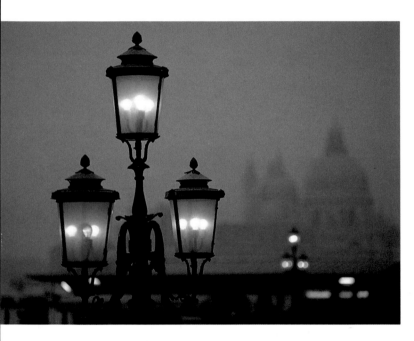

Photo credits:

*Marcello Bertinetti/Archivio White Star:*
Pages 2-3; 7, 10-13; 18-19; 22; 25 top;
28-29; 34 left and top right; 35-39;
41-43; 45 top left; 46 bottom right;
50-57; 66 top, 67-69; 83-89; 94-97;
102-103; 106, 107 left, right, top and
bottom, 108-119; 124-125; 128.

*Carlo De Fabianis/Archivio White Star:*
Page 66 bottom.

*Giulio Veggi/Archivio White Star:*
Cover, back cover; pages 1; 6; 8-9;
14-15; 17; 20-21; 23-25; 30-33;
34 bottom right; 44; 45 bottom left
and top right,: 46 left, 46 top right;
47-49; 58 bottom; 60-65; 70-82;
90-93; 98-101; 104-105; 107 center
right; 120-121; 126-127.

*Luciano Ramires/Archivio White Star:*
Pages 122-123.

*Gianfranco Fainello/Arena di Verona:*
Pages 58 top; 59.

*Lelli & Masotti/Archivio Fotografico
Teatro alla Scala di Milano:*
Pages 4-5.

*Ministero Beni Culturali e Ambien-
tali/Soprintendenza Archeologica della
Calabria:*
Pages 26-27.